The Day the Barn Almost Burned

The Day the Barn Almost Burned

AND OTHER STORIES
OF DEEP SOUTH PLANTATION LIFE
IN THE 1940S

Dickie Williams

3/19/2001

R. B. (DICKIE) WILLIAMS, III

COURT STREET PRESS
Montgomery

Court Street Press
P.O. Box 1588
Montgomery, AL 36102

ISBN 1-58838-014-9

Design by Randall Williams

Printed in the United States of America

To my wife,

my entire family,

and my many friends over the years

Contents

Preface

THIS book is about my early years growing up on my granddaddy's plantation in north Monroe County during the late 1930s and early 1940s.

I was born in Mobile, Alabama, in the old Mobile Infirmary. The Tommy Notion Company employed my father in Mobile. When I was two years old, we moved to Monroeville, which was in the center of my daddy's sales territory and close to home.

My Grandfather Williams had a home in Monroeville and one on the plantation in Finchburg. He and my grandmother would spend the weekends in Monroeville and the weekdays in Finchburg.

My Grandfather and Grandmother Jackson lived in the small community of Tunnel Springs, Alabama. He was in the sawmill business and did small farming.

World War II started, and Daddy was called to serve in the Navy. Mother, my younger brother Robbins, and I moved to Tunnel Springs to live with my mother's father and stepmother, C. J. Jackson and his wife. Every opportunity I had to visit Finchburg, I leaped at it. Most of this was on holidays and in the summers. In the summer my grandfather would come to Tunnel Springs and pick me up on Sunday afternoons, and I would spend the week at Finchburg. I want to point out this is not in any way showing partiality to

My mother's family lived in Tunnel Springs, Alabama. Above left, her father C. J. Jackson. Above right, my step-grandmother, Margaret Tolbert Jackson. Bottom left, my Father's mother, Lucy Portis Williams, better known as Mam. Bottom right, my mother, Maggie Laura Williams.

grandparents, but I am just relating certain periods of my childhood memories.

My family on the Williams side consisted of Granddaddy (Captain Dick), Grandmother (Mam), Aunt Louise (the oldest), Aunt Julia, Daddy, Uncle Fonde, and Uncle Maiben. Uncle Maiben seemed more like an older brother, because we were only a few years apart in age and had the same interests, mainly hunting and fishing.

Aunt Louise and Aunt Julia lived in Monroeville. Aunt Louise taught school, and Aunt Julia supervised the large home in Monroeville. Daddy and Maiben were in the service, and Uncle Fonde lived on the plantation in Finchburg in the first home built in 1830. With Granddaddy supervising, they ran the everyday operations on the plantation.

Above, my Aunt Louise Williams. Right, Aunt Julia Williams.

In the pages that follow, I have tried to give readers a true description of the life on a plantation from the late 1930s through 1946. All of the stories are true, and most are on the comical side; however, there was another side of plantation life that I hope to write about soon.

In the meantime, those of you who were raised on a farm during this era are invited to compare your experiences and memories with mine. The kids raised in towns and cities can read this account and see what they missed.

My brother Robbins and me in the backyard of Grandaddy's home. The Boston bulldog, Nell, lived to the ripe old age of nineteen.

The Day the Barn
Almost Burned

The "Big House," built in the early 1900s
across the road from the "Big Store."

I

The Good Old Days

THE Williams Plantation was located in Finchburg in southwest Alabama, about halfway between Montgomery to the north and Mobile to the south. The plantation was bordered by the Alabama River and extended into the hills and large fields away from the flood plains. The Alabama River would flood the bottom lands at least once and sometimes several times each year, depending on the rainfall, flowing to the south toward Mobile Bay from north Monroe County and Montgomery.

During this time cotton was still king and it dictated how our lives were lived. Most of the cotton was raised on large farms by large landowners known as planters. The planters owned the land and had tenants, most often black families, who lived on the plantation and worked the crop. The Big House, where Granddaddy and Grandmother Williams lived, was located in the center of the plantation. The planter realized, in order to keep a good labor supply, that he needed to furnish the essentials for living in a small community. Each plantation usually had a store or commissary. The store stocked everything: essential staple food items, tools, fertilizers, seed, and even caskets. Very few items were needed that could not be found in the inventory. The store was located in the center of the Williams plantation across the road from my granddaddy's home.

Because of the bookkeeping method that became an integral part of operating the store, a system known as tenant farming began. Each tenant that wanted to participate was assigned forty acres to be farmed. The planter advanced seed, fertilizer, land use, and credit in the store to the tenant, and said a prayer for him that a good crop would be made. At the end of the year, usually in November or December, after the cotton was ginned and sold, the books were balanced and the profits divided. As in all walks of life, some were better farmers and managers than others; however, regardless of a poor crop, no one went without or went to bed hungry.

The homes of the workers were located in all directions from the store. Most of the homes were near the fields that each family farmed except for the workers who were specialized in the operation of the plantation. These included the cooks, the gin operators, the gristmill operators, the tractor drivers, and various workers who reported to Granddaddy each morning. These workers lived near the store on both sides of the road, with the cook's house located close to the big house. The large barn used for boarding horses, mules, and milk cows was located across and down the road from the store.

The cotton gin.

The grist mill.

Since cotton was king, this was the crop that had to be harvested and made ready for the market. This required a cotton gin. Most plantations erected their own gins, mainly because of the poor transportation then available and the monetary gain that could be earned by ginning your own cotton.

The cotton gin was run by steam power fueled by wood burning in a huge boiler. The gin was located several hundred yards up the road from the store and house. The location of the gin was a safety precaution in case the boiler overheated and exploded or the cotton gin caught fire. The cotton warehouse was located across the road from the gin.

Each large farm needed its own gristmill. The Williams gristmill was located below the gin toward the house, but not too close to the house because of the noise and the risk of accidental fire. All those living on the plantation depended on the gristmill for grinding corn into the staple foods of corn meal and grits for daily consumption. The gristmill was usually close to the gin and in many cases was run from the same power source. The gristmill usually operated on

Saturday of each week. The workers, or "hands," as almost everyone called them, always arrived at the gristmill with at least a bushel of shelled corn to be ground into grits and meal. A bushel of corn would last most families a week or more, depending on the size of the family.

No plantation was complete without a sugar cane mill and a sugar cane furnace for making molasses or syrup. The sugar cane grinding mill was located up the road from the store in a field adjoining the cotton warehouse. Syrup-making was a seasonal operation dependent on the maturing crop of sugar cane. Sugar cane was harvested in the fall before the first frost. The cane, stripped of its leaves, left long stalks, which were cut and piled into stacks or loaded onto wagons to go to the mill for grinding and extracting the sweet juice from the stalks.

The sugar cane mill was a simple operation (if you were used to it). Every plantation had one or two hands who specialized in this operation. They made it look so easy. The mill consisted of a grinding machine. The cane was inserted by hand into the rollers, which squeezed out the juice. A mule, harnessed to a long pole that was attached to the grinder, furnished power for this operation. The mule walked in circles all day, with the hand stuffing the stalks of sugar cane into the grinder. At the same time, he tried not to let the overhead pole hit him in the head, and he was very careful that his fingers did not get into the rollers with the cane. Most of the time, a cane mill was a two-man operation, with the worker described above and a second worker who collected the juice as it ran down to a bucket from the grinder. It was the duty of this worker to carry the buckets of cane juice to a waiting wagon loaded with barrels used to transport the juice. His main concern was to keep from getting knocked down by the overhead pole that was connected to the syrup mill.

The wagon driver drove the wagon, loaded with the barrels, to the next phase of the operation—the syrup-cooking furnace. The

A mule walked round and round the cane mill (grinder) providing the power to squeeze out the juice for syrup-making.

furnace was ideally located about a quarter of a mile down the road below the store near a branch with clean water. It was surrounded by abundant timber of all species, which was used as fuel to cook the cane juice. The furnace for cooking the juice consisted of an open-sided roof over a long rock and mortar kiln. A fire was built in this kiln to cook the cane juice. Huge metal pans were inserted into position over the fire. Cooking the juice was a special operation, and very few workers could perform this operation—usually just one person from each plantation. The fire had to be kept just right in order not to burn the juice. The juice was heated, and under watchful eyes of the syrup maker, the operation proceeded. Two to four workers were introduced into the operation to act as skimmers. They used long-handled dippers to scoop the skimmings that rose to the top of the heated juice.

The skimmings were a by-product of syrup making, and were placed into barrels, then made into homemade beer after it had fermented in the barrels for a while. For some strange reason, these barrels often evaporated very soon after the skimmings started to ferment. It was not hard to solve this mystery, especially when a worker did not show up for work the next morning, or sometimes for several days, depending on the amount of skimmings that were missing. I have always been told you have never really been drunk until you get drunk on cane skimmings.

Many hours of sleep were lost during syrup-making time. Once the operation started, it had to continue nonstop until all the juice had been cooked into syrup, which was really the end product.

The sawmill was located down the road from the store near the cane furnace. There was always a supply of lumber for barns, fences, or any other use on the plantation. The surplus was sold to the larger sawmills in the area.

We now have on the plantation the cotton gin, gristmill, commissary, saw mill, and syrup mill. However, no plantation would be complete without a well-planned garden for each household, and the Williams plantation was no exception. In our large garden, we raised peas, corn, squash, tomatoes, okra, cabbage, and greens—all the vegetables we would need for the year. Any excess of summer vegetables was canned for the winter. The meat for the plantation was raised by the planter, with each household having its own milk cow, hogs, chickens, ducks, turkeys or whatever they wanted for their own use.

The hog pen was always filled with fattened hogs for consumption. Since we had no electricity during this period, the smokehouse was vital. Preserving meat was an art that was performed by one or two workers on the plantation. By knowing how to cure meat, they could make sausage, ham, cracklings, lard, and bacon, as well as many other cuts of meat. It could then be salted, smoked, cured, and hung in the rafters of the smokehouse to be used as needed. Most of the butchering was done after the weather turned cold, usually in November. Cows produced milk, butter, and cheese. Some cows were also butchered when needed for the table, and whatever beef

The smokehouse was located behind and to the right side of the big house near the kitchen.

was not eaten fresh was salted down in brine or canned for cooking.

Chickens, turkeys, ducks, and guineas roamed freely around the plantation. Most of the fowl were killed fresh when ready for consumption. Sometimes, this meat was canned when more than needed was taken either by mistake or overkill.

I would be amiss if I did not mention the role that wild game played in the diet of the plantation dweller. The game that was enjoyed—and in many cases was a necessity—consisted of squirrel, wild turkey, deer, rabbits, quail, dove, duck, coon, possum, or whatever birds could be harvested without wasting a shell.

Many large plantations were located near or at least within walking distance of a large stream. These streams served not only as transportation, but provided an outstanding supply of fresh fish and turtles. Most of the fish were caught and used as needed. Some were salted and canned, but this was an exception; it was too easy to catch the fish and eat them fresh.

I hope this will give you an idea about the everyday operation of a cotton plantation. For those of you that were lucky enough to live on a plantation, I hope the following stories will remind you of the "good old days." The rest of you, I hope, can appreciate the humor of these true stories that I will relate to you for entertainment.

Grandaddy Williams and Uncle Fonde Williams in front of Granddaddy's house in Monroeville.

2

Plantation History and Personnel

IN the early 1900s, the Williams commissary and home were built three miles up the road from the original big house. The store was on one side of the road and the house on the other. Over the years, the plantation became diversified. Cotton was not king, but it was still a staple. Other crops were planted, beef cows were added, and hogs were grown for market. Timber was always a part of the income and was increasing in value.

In the late twenties, my grandfather opened the first butcher shop in Monroeville. He used cows from his herd in Finchburg and also bought cows from other farmers.

Uncle Fonde was in charge of the farm operation. As I mentioned, Daddy and Uncle Maiben were in the service. Uncle Fonde had an accident with a tractor, which broke his pelvis and put him in bed for six months. This left only my granddaddy to oversee everything on the plantation, including operating the store. He was not too fond of doing this, mainly because of his inability to walk without arthritis pain in his hips.

This was my first call to help on the farm. I was to help Granddaddy in the store all summer. I will at this time name only the workers with whom I had daily contact. Pig was the main cook. Sarah Lee, the young cook in training, was the daughter of Buck, who never wore shoes, winter or summer. He was in charge of the garden. His wife, Jim Buck, did odd jobs, such as plucking chickens and gathering vegetables. Her two sons were Doe and T. B., my dear friends and playmates.

Doe was two years older than me and was my granddaddy's helper. Wherever he went, Doe went. His main job was opening gates and hot Budweiser beer while they drove over the plantation. For the most part they stayed stuck. It was a joke among the workers that Captain Dick could never slip up on them, because he would get stuck in the first mud hole. You could see him and hear spinning tires from miles away.

Thomas was the main helper. He was able to do anything from driving a tractor, to chauffeuring my great uncle, to taking me hunting, or whatever came up. Manzie was my hunting partner. He was not a good farmer but was one of the best hunters, which meant more to me. We hunted coons at night and everything legal during the day, mostly rabbit, squirrel, and deer.

Center, my hunting companion, Manzie McCall, cleaning deer in front of the big house.

My first cousin Buddy Boy (Fonde Williams, Jr.) was a constant fishing companion.

I loved fishing almost as much as hunting, but I never persuaded Manzie to go fishing with me. I finally asked him why he would not go fishing. He answered, "I don't hunt nothing that don't make a track."

Thomas's wife, Edna, was a fishing partner to all of us boys, T. B., Jimmy Dee, Buddy Boy, Frazer, and myself. The only way we were allowed to go fishing on the river or creek was to get Edna to go with us. This was never hard to do, because she loved fishing almost as much as we did.

Otis and Gilbert were in charge of running the gin and gristmill. Frank, who was the daddy of my housekeeper of forty years, was another jack-of-all-trades and was very dependable until he was offered a drink. Nig was mostly a farmer and coon hunter, a much better coon hunter than farmer. He was one of a few that could go into the river swamp, hunt all night with a flare made of lightwood knots, and not get lost.

Murry, my Uncle Fonde's fox hunting buddy, was a veteran of World War I and was gassed during a battle with Germany. Everyone said it made him crazy; however, I felt he was peculiar, but not crazy. He did convince the army that he was entitled to a pension, which he drew his entire life.

Alma was another fishing guide with whom we were allowed to go to the river. He specialized in throw-line fishing for catfish. A throw-line is fished from the bank. A length of fifteen to sixteen feet of line was tied and anchored on the bank by a branch driven into the mud. A rock or whatever was heavy enough to hold the line while throwing it anchored the end of the line that was to go into the river. To this line five to ten drop hooks spaced a foot apart were tied to the throw-line. Bait included anything from cut-up black snake, worms,

My brother Robbins, with Clarence Bilbray in the background, displaying a huge river cat typical of the fish we caught as youngsters in the Alabama River.

and crawfish, to salamanders. The line was then thrown straight out into the river. The art of this type of fishing was to know just how to throw the line without throwing the bait off. I never knew Alma to throw his bait away.

Eddie was my turkey-hunting guide. Very few blacks in those days were able to call turkeys, or else they never tried. A few were masters and were in much demand as guides. Eddie used a box-type yelper and turkey hen wing bone, both of which were homemade by the user.

Pewee was Eddie's son and was ready to go hunting whenever asked. No matter what I wanted to hunt—dove, quail, turkey, duck, squirrel, or whatever—he was ready.

J. B. was another of Eddie's sons. His specialty was squirrel hunting. J. B. was born with an eye deformity. We referred to his condition as being walleyed. Both eyes were focused all the way to the right. When he pointed to a hard-to-see squirrel, you always followed the way his hand was pointing, because his eyes seemed to be looking in the opposite direction. He was one of the best at spotting squirrels that I have witnessed.

Papa was Manzie's boy, and we never went rabbit hunting without him. He was the best that I have seen in spotting a rabbit in its bed. We could leave the dogs at home, and with Papa's skill, go home with a sack of cane cutters, better known as swamp rabbits.

Claude was also my hunting and fishing buddy. He liked any kind of fishing, but he hunted mostly turkeys. He was the first guide that I ever saw scratch in the leaves with his hand and take his hat and beat his knees to imitate two turkeys fighting. He could also flap his coat and sound just like a hen flying down from their roost.

Jimmy Dee was the son of one of the farm tenants. At our age of ten, he was tall and wore size twelve shoes—when he wore shoes. He loved fishing almost as much as I did and was always ready to go. We would go through some of the most snake-infested brush that existed while traveling to the creek bank. One day I told Jimmy Dee to

Uncle Fonde Williams and Aunt Bonnie Williams.

watch out for snakes. I warned him to be careful and not step on a snake. His answer to me was "to slap them size twelves on his head and keep on going." From that day forward, Jimmy Dee was in front whenever we headed for the creek.

Little Bud was another fishing and hunting companion. He loved to fish for anything, but his hunting was limited to deer run by dogs.

Ned was the bird-hunting guide for the family or guests. He knew where every covey was located. He handled the dogs, and his wife, Elmira, would dress the quail after the hunt.

There were many more people on the plantation that I knew and loved. Some were too old to hunt and fish with me, but they would sit for hours telling me stories of how great the old days were.

My Aunt Barney, the wife of Uncle Fonde, was a great hunter, and many times she and I went into the swamp hunting squirrels and

Uncle Maiben and Aunt Freida Williams

turkeys. In those days, it was not unusual to scatter a flock of turkeys while squirrel hunting. Sitting down, she would call up a gobbler from the scattered flock, and one of us would get a shot.

My Aunt Frieda, wife of my Uncle Maiben, was crazy about fishing, and we went whenever possible. I cannot remember a time that my uncle or I ever beat her catching fish. We always came home with all that we could eat and give away, with Aunt Frieda having caught the majority.

Daddy and Uncle Maiben came home to work on the plantation after the close of World War II, while Uncle Fonde was still getting over his injury. My granddaddy formed the R. B. Williams Company. Daddy was to keep books and run the store, and Uncle Fonde was over all the farming operations. Uncle Maiben was in charge of the cattle and timber. Granddaddy was still in charge overall. After several years, he turned the entire operation over to the boys. He would come over from Monroeville before day every morning to see that everything was going according to his desire. About 10 a.m., he would get in his car and go back to his Monroeville home. He told everyone in town that Uncle Maiben and I could not wait for him to leave. He said as he was going down the lane, he would look in the rear view mirror and see Uncle Maiben with the hoe and me with a can, going to dig worms. You know, we never admitted it, but most of the time this was true.

Left, my father, R. B. Williams (Little Dick). Above, my younger brother, John Williams, who was not born until later.

Opposite page: (top) A. J. Williams, one of my hunting companions; (center) Arlen Stanton, sitting with Little Bud Johnson; (bottom) Thomas Hill (the jack of all trades). When any of the family wanted anything, Thomas was the first one to be selected.

3

My First All-Day Squirrel Hunt

I WILL never forget the first all-day squirrel hunt at Finchburg. I was six years old and had killed my first squirrel at age five while hunting with my mother in Tunnel Springs. It was a cold Saturday morning with our third frost of the season on the ground. The night before, even when I was sleeping, I was dreaming of the day ahead.

At this time we were living with my grandparents in Tunnel Springs. Daddy commuted daily, except Sunday, from Tunnel Springs to Finchburg. This morning was no different except he had one excited son sitting next to him at 3 a.m. as we headed to Finchburg for me to hunt and daddy to work in the store. Daddy had made arrangements with Thomas and his two dogs to be my guide. Thomas lived above the store, so Daddy turned the 1940 pickup into the drive, which was really a dim road, and drove a mile to Thomas's house. I will never forget the smell of burning oil and the truck heater coming from the floorboard of the truck. When I smell burnt oil from a car today, I am still reminded of that day.

Thomas was up and waiting for us. The two dogs were tied to the front fence, and both were as excited about going as I was. Thomas loaded the dogs, and we headed for the big house, where Sarah Lee was preparing breakfast for the crew.

By this time it was about 5 a.m., and the breakfast was almost ready. I was so excited that eating was the last thing on my mind. However, when the plates of hot biscuits, sausage, fried ham, eggs (prepared to your desire), grits, and homemade butter were served, I joined in with the rest. Jams, jelly, and cane syrup were also on the table. The looks and aroma of this good food took my mind off hunting long enough for me to down a glass of milk, two eggs, grits, two sausages, bacon, and two buttered biscuits with jam and jelly. This was not a special breakfast, but an every morning occurrence except for Sunday. Sarah Lee's only rule was not to leave anything on your plate. This was never a concern for me.

Daylight was still thirty minutes in arriving. Daddy insisted that we pack a lunch, and it did not take long for Thomas and me to load a bag with sardines, Vienna sausages, pork and beans, crackers, and Cokes. Daddy also insisted on my taking two boxes of shells and one box for Thomas. Thomas shot a 30-inch single-barrel 12-gauge shotgun. I was shooting my granddaddy's double-barrel 20-gauge Fox.

Most kids my ages were taught to hunt with a single-barrel .410-gauge shotgun. Due to World War II and the scarcity of shells, I had to shoot whatever gun fit the gauge of shells that were available. My own first gun was a single-barrel .410, but shells for this gauge were really hard to find, so I was usually forced to shoot my Grandfather Jackson's double-barrel 12-gauge. But the 20-gauge double-barrel shotgun that belonged to Granddaddy Williams was to be used on this hunt. I was accustomed to the much larger 12-gauge, so the 20-gauge was not hard to adjust to.

Daddy told us to get in the pickup and he would take us pretty close to our hunting grounds, which was two miles down the road. He also let it be known that we would have to walk back to the store after the hunt. My feet had forgotten about the cold.

The smell of smoke coming from the kitchens and fireplaces emitted an aroma that is hard to forget. Daylight was near as Daddy let us out in what we call "the hills." Hunting locations were broken down into two types of terrain, the hills with small streams between them and the swamps or river-bottom terrain. The hunt today would start in the hills, and continue west to the river swamp and riverbank, up the riverbank, and then back to the hills and home.

The dogs were released and the hunt was on. Thomas reached into the back of the pickup and retrieved two burlap sacks, commonly known in these parts as "croaker sacks." One was a shot and game bag, which he hung around his neck. The other bag held our lunches and shells, which was a load in itself.

Daddy was only halfway across the big cornfield in the truck when Old Tom let out a series of barks, just in the woods from the edge of the cornfield. In a few minutes Old Nell gave Tom some help, and the race was on. For ten minutes we listened and in the meantime, it became light enough to walk in the woods. Even though frost was on the ground and the temperature was in the low thirties, we still wanted to see where we were stepping because of rattlesnakes. They are not as active in the cold, but yes, they can still bite and still deserve everyone's respect.

Thomas made the remark that he could not believe a squirrel was running that far and that long without treeing. At that moment, Thomas looked at me and said they had treed. My heart was already beating like crazy from the excitement of the hunt and the anticipation of filling two sacks with squirrels. Both sacks filled with squirrels would be over a hundred count, but keep in mind that an excited young boy of six had all kind of dreams and imaginations. Thomas told me to follow him, and down toward the barking dogs we went. Just as we came out of a thicket, we could see the two dogs barking as they surrounded the base of a bay (magnolia) tree on the bank of a small steam. The tree was huge with many leaves and limbs. Thomas circled the tree looking for the squirrel. Suddenly I could hear Thomas talking to himself, "Darn, what a coon!"

In the next breath, he was calling me to come stand next to him.

Then I heard him say, "I see two coons up there." Thomas was taking every precaution and would only let me load the gun when we were ready to shoot. Uncocking the double barrel, I inserted two 20-gauge shells, size 6 shot, and was now ready to take my first coon. I know now that a coon is really a raccoon, but I was in the sixth grade before I learned the correct spelling. However, I still prefer the spelling of "coon."

Thomas pointed toward a limb near the top of the tree. In a few seconds, I had the coon in my sights and pulled the trigger on the right barrel. Down through the limbs the coon fell. Thomas and the two dogs were on the coon as soon as it hit the ground. As badly as I wanted to see the commotion under the tree, I could not avoid seeing two more coons on another limb. Taking careful aim with the left barrel, I fired again. Before Thomas could recover from the unexpected shot, another coon almost fell on his head. I reloaded quickly, and a well-placed shot brought another coon crashing to the ground. On the other side of the tree, not as high as the others, but on a limb, were two more coons, which I brought down, one with each shot. By this time Thomas and the dogs were dodging falling dead coons instead of trying to catch them. Five coons were on the ground, and one was left in the tree.

Thomas was so busy grabbing coons from the dogs and putting them in the sack that he could not hear me say that there was still another coon left in the tree. I reloaded and fired. The coon moved on the trunk of the tree but did not fall. By this time Thomas had picked up five coons and was catching his breath, as he walked toward me. I told Thomas that the coon acted as if he was wounded but would not fall or move. Thomas took one look and said, "Man, that is one big coon. Shoot him again." Taking careful aim, I fired again. The coon did not move. Thomas instructed me to shoot again. This time the coon went limp, with legs hanging from the trunk of the tree, but still not falling. Thomas looked at me and said that the coon must be hung in the tree.

I had a better view of the situation after walking up the hill a way and looking backward. The coon was dead, but had stuck his head in a hollow hole and become lodged and was not about to fall. I told Thomas we could leave him until we came back at the end of the hunt and maybe by then he would have fallen out. Thomas looked at me and said, "We ain't going to leave that big coon up there," and he proceeded to climb the tree. The tree had many limbs, and the climbing was easy most of the way, that is until he ran out of limbs and was still ten feet from the coon. I was begging him to come down before he fell. I was not as concerned about his safety as I was worried about me getting out of those woods by myself. However, I never let him know my priorities.

Thomas was not about to give up, as he stood on the last limb, with a distance to go before reaching the coon. Now down in the South, we have a skill — not known by many, unless they have seen it performed—called "skinning up a tree." Wrapping your legs and arms around the trunk of the tree performs this act, while pulling upward with the arms and advancing until the desired height is reached. Thomas accomplished this in a matter of minutes, while I was still worried about him falling and leaving me stranded in those woods by myself. Reaching the dead coon and pulling his head from the hole, he dropped the coon to the ground.

The dogs and I got there about the same time with me beating them by a few seconds. Lifting the coon from the dogs, I realized what Thomas had meant when he said, "That's a big coon." When Thomas got on the ground, he relieved me of the chore of keeping the dogs from chewing on the coon. As cold as it was, I could not help noticing sweat all over Thomas's face as he shook the dead twigs and bark from his shirt.

Six coons were placed in one of the sacks. This was a load for a grown-up to carry. I could hardly drag the sack.

Thomas explained that we would tie the sack of coons in a tree and pick them up on the way back, because we had much more hunting to do. Before we had finished tying the sack of coons in the tree, Old Nell gave out a series of barks, and Tom followed with a tree bark. On the way to the tree, I made the statement that I hoped it was a squirrel and not more coons. Thomas wholeheartedly agreed, saying, "Us has already got enough coons for today."

Arriving at the base of a large water oak, where the dogs were leaping at the tree, we started to look for a squirrel. Near the top, on the side of the trunk, was a fat gray squirrel. I took careful aim, and down came the squirrel. As the squirrel was falling through the limbs it created a noise and caused another squirrel to move from his hiding place—giving me a clear shot, adding squirrel number two to our bag.

After retrieving the dead squirrels, I noticed Thomas examining each squirrel before allowing me a look and remarking, "We are going to have a cold winter." After asking what he was talking about, I was told to feel how thick the hide was on the squirrels. All the older folks believed that when wild game had unusually thick coats of fur, it was a sign of a cold winter approaching.

THE TIME was still early, and the sun was beginning to rise. The dogs continued treeing squirrels, some in holes, some in nests, and some easy to see. The second best thing to happen, while squirrel hunting with dogs, was for them to tree a squirrel in a tree with vines running the entire length of the tree. The best squirrel hunting, with a dog, is to be able to get a clear shot without having to look very hard. With the shooter in a good position to view the entire tree, a squirrel in a tree with vines can easily be located by shaking the vines. Usually at the first shaking, the squirrel will jump from its hiding place and this offers a clear shot. Sometimes, as many as five squirrels will be in one tree.

We were fast approaching the high ridge overlooking the river swamp. River swamp hunting is easier hunting than hill hunting and has always been my favorite. The walking is not as bad, because the ground is flat and clean. Most river bottoms have sloughs and wet weather cypress ponds. During this time of year, they hold ducks in abundance, especially if there has been a good acorn crop.

Most of our duck population was made up of wood ducks, called summer ducks by the old hands. This was because they could be seen year round and were thought not to migrate. This theory has since been proven otherwise. The other duck was a mallard, which has been popular in these parts for a very long while. It migrates along the river and heads south at the first sign of cold weather in the northern breeding grounds. Wood ducks and mallards were drawn by the hundreds to the sloughs and ponds, which are surrounded by water oak trees. These trees produce an abundance of acorns that fall into the water and become food for the ducks.

As we descended the large ridge toward the flat river bottom, we could hear the squeal of the wood duck and the quacking of feeding mallards. The noise was coming from an eight-acre wet weather pond, which was full of rainwater and acorns which had fallen from the surrounding trees. My heart started to pound, as I thought my chance of taking my first duck was gone.

As we approached the pond, at least two hundred mallards flushed right in front of me. Out of instinct, I raised my double barrel and fired twice into the rising flock of beating wings. Thomas fired one shot with his single barrel. I saw two mallards fall and was not sure if there were not more.

Even though the ducks had fallen into knee-deep water, the cold and dampness in my leaking pair of ordinary boots did not deter me from retrieving the ducks. Reaching the first duck, with water already over my boot tops, was a thrill I will never forget as I picked it up from the water.

It was a beautiful mallard drake with bright orange feet, which I learned later was a sign of a newly migrated duck from up north. The bright orange feet were the results of feeding in the cold, clear water found up north. The ducks feeding down south for any length

The swamp pond, bordering the Alabama River, where I took my first duck.

of time have dull brown legs and feet, which are due to the mud content in the muddy sloughs where they are feeding. The other duck was a mallard drake, and as I looked across the pond, I could see two more ducks on the water surface. One made a circle with its head down and the other one was still.

I walked back through the water and received a scolding from Thomas for getting my feet wet. With all of the excitement, I had forgotten I even had feet. Laying the two fat drakes on the leaves, I admired the beautiful green heads and the orange feet. Their beauty was hard to put into words.

Thomas was already gathering wood to build a fire, so I could dry my feet. After starting the fire, Thomas added his duck to my two. His was a fat male wood duck so full of acorns you could shake him and actually hear the acorns rattling in his craw. I removed my wet boots and socks and hung them on two sticks near the now warming fire. I related to Thomas that I had seen two more ducks on the water on the other side of the pond. One was wounded and the other dead. Thomas always wore waterproof rubber boots that came to his knees, so he could walk through shallow water without getting his feet wet. I was told not to move from the fire, as Thomas went around the shallow end of the pond to see if he could retrieve my other two ducks.

By this time the dogs had smelled the fire and came to me thinking that there might be some food available. In a few minutes, Thomas called to say he had retrieved both ducks and was coming back to the fire. Both dogs had lain down by me near the warm fire. Thomas, thinking the dogs were still-hunting, began to call them. Old Tom raised his head and quickly went back to sleep. Nell did not move a muscle. I called to Thomas and told him the dogs were with me. Steam was rising from my wet socks and boots as they rested beside the hot fire. My feet started to sting, and I soon realized that they were freezing cold. About this time, Thomas arrived back at the fire with my two other mallards, both of which were drakes. Taking the squirrel sack and wrapping it around my cold feet was a blessing in disguise, because the warm-bodied squirrels and the sack gave me some relief from my now freezing feet.

Thomas added more wood to the fire and joined me to warm his hands. It was hard to believe we had killed five ducks with three shots, but we had the proof. The time was 10:15 a.m., and we were still two hundred yards from the riverbank. Thomas made the statement that as soon as my boots and socks dried; we would head to the riverbank and start hunting. The squirrels had already fed and gone up into the trees. The trees, covered by vines and Spanish moss, stretched for miles along the riverbank, and were draped with squirrel nests.

My boots dried and we were ready to go. We put out the fire and headed for the riverbank. The trees along the riverbank were old, tall, oak trees with plenty of cover for a sleeping squirrel. The dogs started treeing immediately. Most of the time we had to shake the vines to make the squirrels move in order to have a clean shot. Most trees had one or two squirrels in each, with the most in any one tree being five. I did not take long to fill the sack.

It was 11:30 a.m., and the early morning breakfast was wearing off. Sitting under a large moss-covered oak overlooking the Alabama River, we decided to bring out our canned goods and eat dinner. This was a meal that I will never forget. All the time while eating, I could not help but hold one of the mallards and admire its beauty. The sun had warmed the air somewhat, and we almost fell asleep. Maybe we did nod off, because before we realized it, it was 1:30 p.m.

I still wanted to hunt even though Thomas explained that it would be late before we walked the five miles back home. He did console me with the fact that we could hunt all the way back home. What I did not realize was the squirrels had gone up for the morning, and it would be at least 4 p.m., before they began to stir again. Just before leaving the river bottom, Old Tom gave a loud bark, and as I looked his way, a large cane cutter, also known as a swamp rabbit, came running straight toward me. At twenty yards, I fired, adding one more meal to our game sack, which was getting pretty heavy by this time. As we headed toward home, the dogs were tired, Thomas was tired, and I was very tired but would not have admitted it for anything.

Around 4 p.m., we arrived at the tree with the coons, still tied in the sack. It was a load, and I knew that both sacks were too heavy for me to try to lift, so Thomas had to carry both sacks.

After arriving at the large cornfield adjoining the woods, we decided to make a bag check. One sack had six grown coons. The second sack held twenty-nine squirrels, five ducks, and one huge rabbit. The game and shot bag held one can of sardines (three were eaten), and one can of Vienna sausages, of which the original count was five. There were no pork and beans and very few crackers left. Seven 20-gauge shells were left out of the original two boxes. Eighteen 12-gauge shells remained. This will give you a good idea of what was eaten and who did most of the shooting.

This sounds as if we were meat hogs, but you have to realize, none of the game in the bag broke the limit. There was an abundance of game at that time, and we took only a small percentage of the overflowing game. None of the bags of game were wasted. I will never forget what my grandfather and Daddy had instilled in me from day one: that was to obey the game laws and never take game that you were not going to eat or use.

As the sun was setting, we started the long walk back home, crossing the large cornfield. In the center of the cornfield was a large pecan tree, with all the branches bare of leaves, and as I glanced at the tree, I did a double take. I could not believe my eyes. It seemed there was a dove on every twig. The setting sun was bearing down on the huge tree, and the sight reminded me of a Christmas tree.

There had to be at least four hundred doves in that one tree. I started to beg Thomas to let me slip up to the tree and shoot a mess of doves. No way was he going to let me waste any more time, and besides he had all he could carry as it was. We left without disturbing the doves, but I have always wondered how many I could have taken with both barrels.

Never will I forget this hunt. Thomas and I still talk about that hunt and how surprised Daddy was when we emptied the contents of both sacks onto the front porch of the store.

4

The Day the Barn Almost Burned

MY tenure as a store clerk with my granddaddy will always be remembered. T. B. Johnson was my playmate and helper in the store, especially when Granddaddy had to go into town to take care of business. Two seven-year-old clerks left alone in a store full of candy and soft drinks was something to behold. We never asked for any pay because Granddaddy knew we were well compensated by what we were eating and drinking. We would not finish one candy bar before opening another.

World War II was going on at the time and everything was rationed or impossible to get, especially good candies. But for some unknown reason a country store could get all the popular candies it wanted, such as O'Henry, Goo Goo Clusters, Butterfingers, Hershey, Milkyway, Snickers, Baby Ruth, and all brands of chewing gum. The stores in town were limited to very few of these items, and most storeowners kept the good brands for their families. T. B. and I would have qualified as judges for picking the best of all brands, because we tried them all. T. B., at seven, weighed only fifty-six pounds while my weight was 116 pounds. I always accused T. B. of having worms, because he ate just as much or more than I did. He bragged that Captain Dick, as most of the blacks and many whites called my granddaddy, would never believe he ate so much candy because of his weight. He said that I would be the main suspect if candy came up missing since I was the fat one.

A plantation store was never overcrowded with customers; the clerk enjoyed so much spare time. Most customers came early in the morning before going to the fields, and late in the afternoon after working in the fields all day. The store was guarded by an old tomcat that was continually urinating on the sacks of sweet horse and cow feed stacked in one corner of the store. This created wet spots on the feed as well as an aroma that smelled awful, especially during the hot summer months. T. B. and I never did like this cat, because sometimes he either mistook us for a bag of feed or else he meant to urinate on our britches legs. One day during the hot summer, my granddaddy left us in charge of the store, telling us to not get into anything as he left for town. He said he would be back late that afternoon. Before he was out of sight, we were both in the candy counter, trying one of each brand of candy and sometimes more. After eating all the candy we could hold, we retired to our favorite resting place on top of the sacks of sweet smelling feed; that is unless we found that Old Tom had been there before us. As the sun warmed the feed through the window, it was not hard to smell if Old Tom had been there. Most of the time he had visited several sacks.

T. B. and I decided while we were alone that we would get rid of Old Tom, and do everyone a favor. We did not want to kill him, but just make him run away. We were lost for a solution until T. B. remembered his uncle telling him how he got rid of an egg-sucking dog. He had tied gas soaked rags to his tail and set the rags on fire. They never saw the dog again, but an egg-eating dog showed up at a tenant house four miles down the road with some half burned rags tied to his tail.

If this had worked on a dog, we just knew it would work on a cat. T. B. drained a cup of gas from the old handle which operated the gas pump. I cut a wad of cloth from a bolt of material, which was sold by the yard and used for making clothing. After making a ball from the cloth, we attached a string to it with a loop on the other end for attaching to the cat's tail. The ball was saturated in the cup of gasoline. Next was to find the cat and attach the string with the gas-soaked rags to his tail.

The cat was not hard to find, because we knew that his favorite hiding place was behind the stack of sweet feed. We knew better than to set the rags on fire in the store, so to lure the cat outside, we opened a can of Eat-Well sardines, which could be smelled for several hundred yards. We then placed it on the ground in front of the store. The smell of sardines was too much for Old Tom, and he came running. When he started to eat, we eased up behind him and slipped the string around his tail. Old Tom never noticed, for he was eating his favorite meal, that is, until I struck the match and lit the rags. Old Tom jumped straight up, let out several frightening cat squalls, turned around several times, and took off down the road. The faster he ran the more the flames from the ball of rags burned. The last time we saw that cat, he was going over the barn gate, heading straight into the barn, which was filled with freshly baled hay.

Well, this part we never expected, because we thought he would continue to run down the road like T. B.'s uncle's egg-eating dog and consequently never be seen again.

T. B. looked at me and said, "What's us going to do?"

I said, "I'm going just as far as I can from the barn into the cornfield and wait for it to burn down." By doing this, we could always tell Granddaddy the barn caught fire, and we shut the store and took off down the road, fearful that we might get burned.

We slammed the store door closed and started running through the tall, green corn stalks, which seemed like several miles, but was only several hundred yards. The time was 12:30 p.m. by my Waterbury wristwatch, which was my Santa Claus present the past Christmas. We kept a constant surveillance on the barn, waiting for flames and smoke to rise any minute. All afternoon we waited, but to

The barn that almost burned.

our surprise nothing happened. The sun was starting to set, and we knew we had to get back to the store before Granddaddy arrived from town. We started walking very fast toward the barn to find out what had happened to that fire-tailed cat.

In the back of the barn was a concrete water trough filled with water for the horses. In one corner of the barn was a scared, wet cat with a piece of string still around his tail. Upon further inspection, we located the half-burned wad of rags floating in the mule water trough. Grabbing the rags and burying them outside of the barn did not take too long, because we thought we heard Granddaddy's old yellow pickup coming down the lane. Running as fast as we could, we arrived back in the store just in time to open the door, grab two brooms and start sweeping, just as Granddaddy walked through the door.

I will never forget his first words that afternoon. "Why are you two sweating so much?" We were quick to hold the brooms out in front of us, telling him how hot it was sweeping that big store. His only words were that he was proud we had decided to do a little work around the place.

As for Old Tom, he never came back into the store and could be seen around the barn for years. We learned our lesson, and never again did we ever harm an animal with fire.

The horses would not drink the water, because there was a strong scent of gas coming from the trough. Thomas, the jack-of-all-trades, whose job included watering and tending the horses, questioned us. We even went down to the barn with Thomas and swore that we could not smell gas, even though there was a film floating on top of the water in the trough. We finally convinced Thomas and Granddaddy that what they had smelled was rat poison, which had, been placed in the barn. We do not know if they really believed us, but the subject was dropped, and T. B. and I have never mentioned this day to anyone.

However, for many months, I had nightmares about the day we almost burned down the barn. For months afterwards, I could not help staring at that old barn and thanking the "Man" upstairs for sparing us.

5

Killing the Thanksgiving Turkey

MY great-uncle, a bachelor, lived in the big house. His name was Lawrence Williams, but the family called him Uncle Buddy. He was my granddaddy's half-brother and was asked to move in with the family, because he was not able to make a living on his own. It was easy to see why he could not make it on his own. There was just no demand for a full-time hunter or fisherman, or at least, there was no money in it. If he was not fishing, he was hunting. Now, I do not see anything wrong with this, but an income had to be made.

Granddaddy outlined Uncle Buddy's duties on the plantation. He was to oversee the care and feeding of the horses, oversee the garden, and supervise the gathering of the vegetables.

The garden job was one of his favorites, because it required little effort. It consisted of Thomas placing a chair at the end of each row, and moving it as the plantation hands moved from one row to another. He always walked with the help of a stick. Buck, the main worker in the garden, always said Captain Buddy could spot a green twig of grass in a row a hundred yards away. The only time I ever witnessed him moving his own chair, was the morning Thomas sat his chair down over an anthill. Uncle Buddy moved his chair up several rows and never limped as he usually did. He always did accuse

Granddaddy of telling Thomas to place his chair over the anthill.

Uncle Buddy always kept a new, well-cared-for four-door Buick in the garage. It was well-cared-for because Thomas washed and cleaned it twice a week. Thomas was also Uncle Buddy's chauffeur, since Uncle Buddy never learned to drive.

Early every Sunday morning, he and Thomas would depart from Finchburg in the well-polished and well-washed car. His destination was to visit all the neighbors, especially the families that had unmarried females. He made his rounds for miles around, sometimes visiting as many as eight families on any one Sunday. You could always tell the family with the best cook, because he and Thomas arrived at this particular house just before the noon meal. I have been told Uncle Buddy was a ladies' man and probably had a few children: however, all I can remember of his skills were horse-back riding, hunting, and fishing.

One morning Grandmother (Mam) wanted a turkey killed for the upcoming Thanksgiving meal, which was always held at the big house in Monroeville. It was observed at noon on Thanksgiving Day, with all the immediate families present.

Granddaddy always let the flock of turkeys roam freely, except when one was needed for eating. The turkeys were then driven into a holding pen until the next morning. Usually, before daybreak, Thomas was given a single-barrel shotgun with one shell, in order to harvest the selected turkey. Just at daylight, he would pick the bird of choice and take him with one shot, never hitting anything but the head. This particular morning was cold, and Thomas had been sent to the swamp long before daylight to check on some cows. Mam did not want to wait for Thomas to return to kill the turkey, so she woke Uncle Buddy from a heavy sleep. She told him he was to go and kill the turkey because Thomas was not there.

Uncle Buddy always slept in long-handle underwear that had a flap in the back for convenience, especially on cold mornings.

Still half asleep, he decided to go in his underwear, get the job

Turkeys in holding pen.

done and then get back into the warm bed. Uncle Buddy grabbed his old double-barrel rabbit-eared shotgun and headed toward the turkey pen. The cold was eating him up, especially in the area the flap was supposed to cover.

By the time he reached the turkey pen, it was light enough to see, so he loaded the old double-barrel with two shells. He picked out a nice bird and took good aim. Just as he was ready to pull the trigger, Old Tip, our bird dog, stuck his cold nose to the part of Uncle Buddy that the flap was supposed to be covering. Both barrels went off, with Uncle Buddy jumping halfway through the fence. Nine turkeys were flopping, either dead or dying: two were hung in the fence from being scared to death.

He was afraid to let my grandmother know what he had done, but the cold was biting, and he knew Sarah Lee was on the way to get the turkey in order to start dressing it. Uncle Buddy passed Sarah Lee in a hurry, instructing her that the turkey was dead in the pen. What he did not tell her was there were nine and maybe two more ready for picking. Sarah Lee made several trips retrieving the turkeys and taking them to the kitchen for dressing. Uncle Buddy had just crawled back under the warm blankets, when he heard Mam scream as she walked into the kitchen and saw the pile of dead turkeys.

Uncle Buddy dressed as quickly as he could and tried to slip out without being seen. This did not work because Granddaddy insisted that Uncle Buddy eat breakfast before going wherever he was going in such a hurry. Uncle Buddy did not have much choice but to return to the dining room.

By this time, Granddaddy had peeped into the kitchen and could not believe what he saw—eleven unplucked turkeys lying on the floor with shots scattered from their heads to their feet. One of Mam's rules was that you never shot a turkey anywhere except in the head and none of the eleven qualified.

Now, the bad part of this ordeal was, we did not have refrigeration at that time, and what we killed had to be eaten or preserved in some way, which was done by smoking it in the smokehouse, canning it, or salting it down in brine in a wooden barrel. All of this took the whole day, with Uncle Buddy helping to pick the turkeys, by orders of Granddaddy. Until the day of his death, he was never asked nor did he volunteer to kill the Thanksgiving turkey again.

Old Tip, the bird dog who helped Uncle Buddy harvest the Thanksgiving turkey.

6

A Snake in the Corn Crib

ONE cold, freezing December morning, as we sat at the breakfast table, Granddaddy suggested that Buck and I hitch up the wagon. We were to go three miles down the road from the store to a large field planted with corn and grain sorghum. A corncrib stood in a stretch of woods near the field and was filled with unshucked corn. Buck's job was to crawl inside the crib and shuck the corn. My assignment was to go to the sorghum field and kill a mess of doves. This was one job that I loved, and Granddaddy knew it.

Buck and I rode the wagon down the cold, dark road for what seemed like three hours. As stated before, Buck would not wear shoes in the winter or summer. It hurt me to look at those cold, black feet when my feet were fairly warm, because I was wearing three pairs of socks inside my boots. At any rate, Buck preferred going barefooted. At last, with teeth chattering from the cold wagon ride, we arrived at the field. It was getting daylight, and I could hear the sound of doves coming to feed in the grain field. Buck drove the wagon to the middle of the field, and helped me get my gun and shells together. I did not know if I was shaking from excitement or was freezing or both. As I stepped on the frozen rows of grain sorghum, the ice cracked under my feet. Buck said, "You be careful and when I fill these two cotton baskets with shucked corn, I'll be back to pick you up."

The corncrib was a tall, one-room building, with a high door. Planks or boards (called either, depending on where you were raised) were nailed across the opening to keep the corn from falling out. One particular board was always loose, and could easily be removed from the opening without prying the nails from the board. This was used as the entrance to the crib. The corn was piled from the ceiling to the floor in a sloping stack, which leaned toward the door. Hanging on the bare wall was a hoe, which was used to rake the shucks away from the unshucked corn. It was also used to pull more corn from the top of the pile down toward the shucker for easy reaching. The shucks were discarded around the worker's feet, mainly for convenience, and I believe, also to keep their feet warm.

I was shooting doves as fast as a pair of frozen hands could reload. It was so cold the doves could hardly get off the ground, so if I missed one coming in, all I had to do was walk it up and shoot again. Most of the time the range was ten to twelve yards. If I delayed five minutes in retrieving the birds, they became frozen stiff where they hit the ground. The sun was now appearing over the tree line, which adjoined the field. It made me think the sun was giving off some heat, but my hands and toes told another story.

Just as the doves really started to pour in, I heard the worst noise I have ever heard coming from the corncrib. Boards were being ripped off, and the worst screaming and hollering I have ever witnessed, spread across the large fields. With my gun in hand, I began to race toward the corncrib. On the way, all I could imagine was that a large rattlesnake had bitten Buck, and he was taking the nearest way out, which was through the side of the crib. As I arrived, boards were still flying from the side of the crib and finally out rolled Buck, with his hoe still in his hand and yelling to the top of his voice.

Running toward him, I could see blood squirting from the area of his big toe. I was scared to death, since I was young and

The corn crib, with missing boards where Buck made his exit.

inexperienced with this type of situation. Still not knowing what his problem was, I finally got him calm enough to tell me what was wrong. It seems that after shucking a large pile of corn and discarding the shucks over his bare feet, all of a sudden there appeared a large black head from beneath the pile of shucks covering his feet. With both hands, Buck grabbed the hoe, and tried with all his strength to cut off the snake's head. The hoe did its job, but the head of the snake happened to be Buck's big toe, which explains what happened to him that cold morning.

Still scared to death, I found an empty fertilizer sack and wrapped Buck's bleeding foot tight as I could. We loaded ourselves in the wagon, and headed for the store as fast as we could make the mules go. Buck was hollering all the way. I guess what kept him from bleeding to death was the cold, and the compress of residue fertilizer, which was still in the sack. Granddaddy sent Buck to Dr. R. A.

Dr. R. A. Smith, Sr., who sewed Buck's toe back on.

Smith, Sr., our family doctor in Monroeville, who sewed up what was left of Buck's toe.

This was some way of ending a great dove shoot. Even today, when I pass that old corncrib, which is still standing with several boards missing from its side, I recall that freezing morning—when Buck thought he had killed a huge black-headed snake.

7

The Wagon Was Too Wide

ALMA was our fishing companion and all of us kids were allowed to go to the river in his care. We would load up in Alma's one-mule wagon and head for the river early in the mornings. The river was three miles from Alma's house, so we enjoyed the wagon ride. Along the trail, we were always looking for catalpa worms on the trees that grew along the fencerow. Catalpa worms are caterpillars that thrive, and get fat from eating the large green leaves of the catalpa tree. They always appear in cycles, and were not always available for fish bait. But when they are available, these worms are one of the best fish baits, especially for use on throw lines when fishing for catfish in the river. We were lucky this particular morning; the third tree we checked was full of grown worms. We all quickly unloaded, started to pick the worms and placed them in a croaker sack for later use. Further down the dirt road, a black snake slithered across the road. Alma stopped the wagon, grabbed his walking stick, killed the snake, and added him to the bait bucket. I had never seen a snake used for catfish bait until now.

As we started down the long hill, before getting to the river bottom, Alma informed us we only needed some crawfish and puppy dogs (salamanders) to complete our supply of bait. He said

Alma's mule, which pulled the wagon that carried us to the
Alabama River for a day of fishing.

this bait could be found in an old half-dry swamp pond, just off the road before we would get to the river. The only danger was the cottonmouth moccasins, and we were warned to look out for them. We turned off the road, and headed the wagon toward the pond. Each boy had a syrup bucket to hold his bait. After turning over rotting, wet logs, we soon had a good supply of salamanders. Fortunately, none of us were snake bit and we continued to gather our bait. The only thing left to do was gather the crawfish.

Alma produced a homemade drag constructed of screen wire attached to a long stick, which was dragged through the mud holes. Each time we caught all sizes of crawfish. With plenty of bait, Alma drove the old mule toward the riverbank. Just before we entered the old river bank road, the mule stepped on a rotten stump. All heck broke loose as Alma started hollering, "Whoa, mule!"

It was too late. A swarm of yellow jackets emerged from the stump and settled between the mule's back legs. The old mule lit out in high gear, still pulling the wagon, with us hanging on for dear life. Then he decided to go between two trees. The mule cleared the trees, but the wagon didn't. It was too wide and we collided with both trees, just inside of the front wheels. The mule kept on going as he left the wagon and us wedged between the two trees, with the front wheels touching the back wheels. The last time we saw that mule, he was kicking up his heels, braying and still running through the swamp, with the harness and wagon tongue still attached.

We survived with a few scratches and bruises, and needless to say, a canceled fishing trip. Alma was worried about his old mule, but I did not care if I never saw him again.

After a long hot walk back to Alma's house, guess who was standing under the pear tree when we finally arrived? You got it! That old mule with the harness and wagon tongue still attached.

8

The Moccasin in the Mudhole

ONE hot afternoon we were sitting on the old store porch, wondering what we could do next for entertainment. Granddaddy suddenly called out to Doe to get the pickup and to be sure it had plenty of gas—every time one of his vehicles left the store, it was always checked for gas. T. B. and I were told to get the gun and some shells. By the time we arrived back at the porch with the gun and shells, Doe had filled the pickup with gas and driven it to the store porch. Granddaddy was always sitting on the bench with his legs crossed or in his rocking chair with his walking stick in his hand. He gave Doe instructions to drive us down to the large mud hole in the middle of the road, which was located in the middle of a big cornfield. He did not have to tell us what our mission was. We had already seen the huge cottonmouth moccasin many times before in the mud hole, and knowing how much Granddaddy hated snakes, it was not hard to figure out our mission.

"Go kill that snake that ducks underwater every time a car approaches and do not come back until you do," Granddaddy said.

All three of us were thrilled to death to get to ride in the pickup by ourselves, and to be sent on such an important mission. As we approached the mud hole, it was not hard to see the big, dark head that belonged to the large snake protruding from the muddy water.

By the time we got out and loaded the gun, the snake went underwater. We waited several minutes before the snake stuck his head up above the water again. Just as I took aim, back under the water he went.

This went on all afternoon, and we were getting tired of it, so we went back up the road to a strip of woods. With an old ax, we chopped a long water oak pole with all the limbs still attached and decided to use it to rake the snake from the mud hole. This would then give me a clear shot. We pulled the limb for two hours through the mud hole, in every known direction, and still there was no sign of the snake. The sun was beginning to set, so out of desperation we decided to take the pickup and drive back and forth through the mud hole, hopeful that we might run him out or wound him. Doe was driving, and T. B. and I were in the back of the truck with the gun. The center of the mud hole was deep enough to almost touch the running boards. After several trips through the water, with no results, Doe decided to speed up and hit the mud hole at a much faster pace. Water went everywhere, including all over the pickup truck's motor and drowned it out, right in the middle of the mud hole. Still no snake, but we all realized that we were in the middle of the snake's habitat with a dead engine.

T. B. and I were already checking for any holes in the pickup body, which would be large enough for a snake to crawl through. Doe was not about to open the front door.

T. B. and I took no chances and crawled on top of the truck cab. We bumped on the cab to get Doe's attention, just long enough to ask him if there were any holes in the floorboard of the truck. He had not even thought about this, and all we could hear was Doe checking the entire cab of the pickup for holes large enough for a snake to enter.

We waited about thirty minutes before Doe decided to try and crank the truck. At last . . . it sputtered and started. What a relief for all, as Doe drove about a hundred yards below the mud hole before stopping. Our only hope was to crawl within firing range and see if the snake would stick his head up again. Doe remained behind, checking the undersides of the truck, making sure that the snake had not crawled into the under carriage of the truck. With my gun in hand, and T. B. following closely, we crawled to within gun range of the mud hole. All of a sudden, T. B. whispered, "Yon hees," which means he had spotted the target. Just as he started to point in the snake's direction, I saw that large head in the middle of the mud hole. Taking careful aim, I pulled the trigger. Water, snake and mud filled the air. We ran to the mud hole and could see the snake's yellow belly turning over and over. By this time, Doe had joined us and was very relieved to see the snake churning over and over in the water.

We retrieved the oak limb with its thick branches, and Doe began to rake the snake out of the water. T. B. and I stood back, just in case, with the gun loaded. The snake was dead but still moving, even though his head was completely gone. We were three happy boys and could not wait to show him to Granddaddy. We put the snake in the pickup's body and headed for the store. Granddaddy was still sitting on the porch with his legs crossed and leaning on his walking stick. Doe drove right up in front of the porch. T. B. and I had decided on the way home, to surprise Granddaddy by throwing the carcass of the dead snake onto the porch in front of him, so he could admire it. We threw the snake, and Granddaddy threw his stick and said many choice words. I will let you imagine what they were.

He made Thomas cut a switch from a nearby peach tree, and T. B. and I received one of the worst whippings that I can ever recall getting. After rubbing our behinds, we asked Thomas why we got a whipping for killing a snake that Granddaddy told us to kill. Thomas began laughing and said, "You don't ever show Captain Dick a snake, dead or alive, and you sho' don't throw it under his feet."

It seems that one day when Granddaddy was young, he was hoeing in the garden and was almost bitten by a rattlesnake. He chopped the snake's head completely from its body, except for a few inches of his neck that was still attached. Proud of what he had done, he stuck his bare foot in front of the snake's head and said, "Now bite me." The snake did exactly that. It latched onto his big toe. The toe swelled, turned blue, then black, and after several weeks finally healed. From that day forward, Granddaddy did not want to see another snake, poisonous or not, dead or alive.

If we had only known! We were so proud of our kill that we just had to show Granddaddy. Never again would we throw a snake, dead or alive, at anyone. However, several days later we could not keep from laughing at the thoughts of Granddaddy's expression when that snake rolled under his feet.

9

The Annual Cattle Sale

ONCE each year the cattle were rounded up and separated according to the number that was to be sold. The desired cattle were placed in holding pens for loading onto trucks. Most of the time, this was a two- or three-day affair. Granddaddy always sold to Capital Stockyards in Montgomery. Their prices were better, and they would send trucks down to pick up the cows for free delivery to the stockyards. A letter sent to the stockyard a week in advance would result in four or five trucks coming to Finchburg for the pick up.

Most of the trucks, in those days, had open cabs or no cabs. The trucks took at least five hours to return to Montgomery after loading. On this particular trip, the truck drivers decided to arrive at night, sleep until just before day, and get an early start. Sure enough, the five-truck convoy rolled in after dark, just as we finished supper. Granddaddy said, "Come on into the kitchen and have some buttermilk and cornbread."

The five drivers and their helpers asked where they could park the trucks. Granddaddy told them to park under the huge oak trees in front of the house, and they could sleep in them until daylight. All ten men were anxious to get to the kitchen and get a stomach full of buttermilk and cornbread. They all sat down, and Granddaddy told

Sarah Lee to bring the Jug (not the buttermilk jug) and some glasses from the closet.

Granddaddy said to the men, "I know that you had a long ride, so let's have a little drink to kind of relax us before the hard day ahead. The only stipulation is that if my wife starts back this way, down the drink because she can't stand the sight of whiskey."

All agreed and looked on with anticipation of enjoying a good drink. Sarah Lee brought the glasses and the gallon of pure home-made whiskey to the table. It was clear as water and very smooth. All glasses were filled from the jug, and the gallon jug was placed under the kitchen table. Everyone took a swallow of the clear whiskey and commented on how good it was. At this moment Granddaddy yelled, "Drink it down! Here comes Miss Lamb!" This was the name my Grandfather used to address my Grandmother. Our help also addressed her by this same name. All glasses were emptied and Granddaddy, with a faked sigh of relief, refilled the empty glasses. The same warning was given again, and the glasses again were emptied.

Two full glasses of moonshine was the best sleeping medicine available at that time . . . provided you could make it to the bed. Granddaddy insisted they all have a drink of buttermilk, stalling them long enough so Thomas and Buck could get them in the front seats of their trucks for a good night's sleep.

Granddaddy failed to tell the drivers about the flock of turkeys that ran loose on the place during the day and roosted in the large oaks in front of the house every night. Before daylight the drivers were halfway awakened by something falling from the skies. One driver commented to his assistant that those were the largest rain-drops that he had ever felt, then turned his head and fell back into a deep sleep.

Just before daylight, Granddaddy sent Thomas to awaken the drivers, who were still half-drunk and covered with turkey manure, as were the entire cabs of the trucks. This was one mess, so Thomas pointed them toward the well before going back into the kitchen, telling them to go and clean up before Captain Dick saw them. Still half-asleep and drunk, they wobbled toward the well to try and clean up. Thomas told Granddaddy about the mess outside and said he ought to be ashamed of himself. Trying not to laugh, Granddaddy only said, "They asked me for a place to sleep, and I thought of how nice it would be for them to rest under the oak trees."

"You know," he told Thomas, half-laughing, "I forgot about those turkeys roosting overhead. Go tell them to hurry and clean up and come into the kitchen for breakfast."

All thanked him, but they were not about to go back into the kitchen. This was where all the trouble had started, and if it were left up to them, this would be their last trip to Finchburg. By ten o'clock that morning, the cows were loaded, and the men had cleaned up and were sober enough to head for Montgomery. Everything was fairly clean, except for the black-bodied trucks, which were splattered with white and green turkey manure.

Several days later Granddaddy received a letter containing a check and a note asking Captain Dick what in the world had happened to the drivers and their trucks. Some of the drivers were still red-eyed and sleepy that night, when they arrived back in Montgomery and the trucks were a mess. A written reply was sent to Capital Stockyards:

> Dear Sir:
>
> I guess the drivers caught whatever is going around down here.
>
> It makes you red-eyed and unable to walk a straight line. As to the trucks, I can't imagine what those drivers ran into.
>
> Your friend,
>
> R. B. Williams, Sr.

10

Extra Spending Money

TIMES were hard, and the tenants were barely making a living by farming, so Granddaddy gave each of the tenants permission to make a little white lightning for sale, if they wanted to, provided they did not get caught in the process. This was another way of making enough money to feed their family throughout the year. Some tenants were really good in this part-time work, and the town folks sought their whiskey. It did not take long for the best makers to become known. You could recognize them by the number of cars stopping in their front yards on Saturday evenings and nights. The best moonshine makers usually sold out before dark on Saturday. Each gallon sold for two to three dollars. This seemed cheap, but consider that sugar was three cents a pound, and the corn was almost free. Time was the most expensive part of the operation. The income from these small operations fed and clothed many large tenant families.

Every branch with good running water had from one to three liquor stills. Most consisted of three barrels to ferment the corn and a copper still for distilling the liquor. Some used a cheaper still made of galvanized pipe and tanks, which were later found to be the source of lead poisoning which contaminated the whiskey. Many of our old people who drank this lead-contaminated whiskey are either dead or on dialysis treatment, because their kidneys have been severely damaged from the lead. The barrels were filled halfway with corn, sugar, and water, and then left to ferment. This concoction was called "buck."

It was not unusual to find possums and coons drowned in the buck barrels. The carcasses were removed and the buck was still used with the secret being kept. Besides, the liquor was going to be distilled into clear liquid, and its previous condition would be unknown to the consumer. After two drinks it did not make any difference how it was made or how clean the buck barrels were.

Most of the whiskey makers worked at night, so it did not interfere with their farming. When the buck started fermenting and was ready for distilling, many nights were spent on the branches, by the stills, with a warm fire burning while the buck was cooking. Usually an old coonhound or a dog that barked was tied to a tree for a warning in case a stranger tried to make an appearance. If the dog barked, the fire was put out, and the workers untied the dog and ran in the opposite direction and immediately started coon hunting. Very seldom did anyone get caught at the still, but axes and revenue agents destroyed many stills. One unwritten rule of the bootleggers was to never drink what you made because it was really easy to drink up all of the profit.

Gilbert, the gin and gristmill worker, was a good example of what kind of trouble could be caused by drinking your own whiskey. Not only did Gilbert drink, but his wife, Lucy, could outdrink him. She stayed drunk for most of the day, except the days when she walked to the creek to fish, and even then she carried a bottle with her. Lucy always caught fish and was not hard to locate on the creek because of her loud laughing and her drunken singing. Gilbert never could figure where all of his whiskey was going because he never saw Lucy drinking. He was gone all day, and when he came home, Lucy was asleep. She was a daytime drinker, and many times we boys would pass Lucy's house and she was either passed out on the front porch or was singing as loudly as she could.

One night Gilbert had worked late at the gristmill and decided to have a few drinks before going home. Around eleven o'clock Gilbert sobered up enough to stagger from the mill to his house. He lived just down the road from the store. Lucy had long been asleep, and Gilbert was starving. He stumbled into the kitchen and decided to make some biscuits, even though he was still drunk. In this state Gilbert got a bowl full of what he thought was flour and made a large plate of biscuits and ate most of them. The next morning Lucy found Gilbert on the kitchen floor moaning and unable to move. She ran to the store and told Granddaddy what had happened. Granddaddy immediately gave Thomas the truck key and ten dollars and told him to get Gilbert into the truck and take him to the doctor. The only hospital in the area was Carter's Hospital in the small town of Repton, eight miles from Monroeville. Thomas took Gilbert to the hospital, and Dr. Carter diagnosed his problem as poison, with no explanation as to what kind.

Gilbert was sent home to die because in those days, there was no treatment for poison which had been in a person's system overnight. When Thomas arrived back at Gilbert's home, Lucy was drunk on the front porch. Thomas carried Gilbert in and put him to bed. By now Gilbert had begun to come out of his coma and beg for water. Thomas went into the kitchen to get the water and noticed a trail of white powdered residue across the kitchen floor.

The trail led into a back closet where the cotton poison was stored. The spilled poison on the floor solved the mystery as to what had poisoned Gilbert. He had mistaken the cotton poison for flour and used it for the biscuits.

Gilbert was bedridden for two months before being able to walk again, and he had a very noticeable limp until his death. This episode broke up Gilbert's drinking. He still made whiskey, but to my knowledge, he never tasted another drop.

Granddaddy had just purchased two high-priced Black Angus

bulls for breeding purposes. The first night on the plantation they went missing. We formed a search party, and for two days we checked every branch head or thicket on the place. The third morning of searching was a success. Both bulls were found down in a branch and were unable to get up. Eight workers with ropes, pulling on them with all their might, finally got one of the bulls up and walking, not straight but at least up.

Thomas made the comment that the bulls acted drunk and there was a strong smell of fermenting corn on their breath. Two hundred yards up the branch was Gilbert's still, with two of the buck barrels overturned. The bulls had overturned the buck barrels and had eaten and drank all of the mash they could hold. This made them so drunk they rolled all the way down the hill into the branch. We saved one, but the other bull died from pneumonia. From that day forward, when a still was erected, the first thing that was built was a fence that enclosed both the still and buck barrels.

II

The Federal Grand Jury

ONE fall the federal revenue men made a raid without notifying the county sheriff, and eleven of the tenants were arrested and charged with distilling illegal whiskey. The trial was to be held in the Federal Courthouse in Mobile during the first week in November, with Federal Judge McDuffie presiding.

Granddaddy and Judge McDuffie were very close friends, but there was too much evidence to even try to get these cases thrown out of court. He told the court that these men were his main tenants and if they were sent off to prison, the crops would not be planted and the families would starve. The trial was held, and all were found guilty. The sentencing date was set for the first week in March. I do not think any of the accused had any idea how serious a federal charge could be. The only court they had ever been involved with was the county, and Captain Dick always took care of that with the county judge. Most of the time they were only fined, which he gladly paid. This federal court was something different, and the sentence was probation or up to three years, which would be served in prison.

On Sunday, before the sentencing was to be handed out on Monday, Granddaddy sent for all of the defendants and their wives. He wanted them to come to the back porch of the big house because he needed to talk with them.

Thomas took the big truck with high sides on the body and opened the back tailgate to pick up each defendant and his wife. Granddaddy was sitting in his favorite chair on the sun-drenched back porch (actually located on the side of the house). Even though spring was just around the corner, the wind still had a cool bite to it, so the warm sun was welcome.

Thomas drove the truck up the drive to the back gate in front of the porch. All eleven accused tenants, along with their wives, jumped from the back of the large truck and stood in front of Captain Dick. First he tried to instill in them how serious the charges were, and unless they did as he told them to do, they would not have a chance to get out of serving time. The time would be served from March forward, which was just the time of year they were needed the most to plow and plant the fields.

Granddaddy instructed the wives to gather up all the children and dress them, regardless of age, in the worst-looking, worn-out

A raid on one of the many whiskey stills located in the area.

clothes they owned. Most families had from five to eleven children, with ages ranging from six months to twelve years old. The wives and husbands were to do the same, with those that could stand the cold going barefooted. All were instructed to be ready and dressed when Thomas came by to pick them up on the day of sentencing. He would drive them to the Federal Courthouse in Mobile, which was a three-hour drive. They were also told to separate all children with runny noses and colds, regardless to whom they belonged. They were to sit on the front row with three of the wives sitting with them. Each child was given a piece of flour sack for a handkerchief, even if he or she did not know what to do with it. They were to hold it and every now and then cough, whether they had to or not.

The night seemed short and at breakfast Thomas was asked to get the truck and fill the back with several scattered bales of hay, so the kids and women could sit on it. Granddaddy told Thomas to pick up the wives and kids and head to Mobile to the federal courthouse. Granddaddy and Doe, with five of the defendants in the car, were to go ahead and arrive at the courthouse ahead of the truck.

However, before leaving, Granddaddy informed Thomas that he would stand up and stretch in the courtroom, when it was time for him to lead in the wives, children and remaining defendants. He wanted all of them to be seated as a group.

The court was called to order, and sure enough things were going according to Granddaddy's plan. Judge McDuffie asked for the defendants to stand. Only five of the eleven stood, and the Judge asked where the other six were.

Granddaddy stood up from the front row and said, "Judge, the other six are together in a truck and are already late. I'm sure they must have a flat tire, but I'm sure they will be here soon." Granddaddy stood up again and tried to ask the Judge a question. The Judge yelled at the top of his voice, "Captain Dick, will you please approach the bench when you have something to say to me. That's an order."

This is the big truck, here after being used for a deer hunt, that carried the families to the Federal Court in Mobile.

Granddaddy, thinking to himself, "What in the hell has come over John because we have always been close friends." However, he did as he was told and asked the Judge for permission to approach the bench. His wish was granted. Stalling for time, he barley made it to the bench with the aid of his faithful walking stick. The Judge asked Granddaddy what he wanted.

"Judge, I sure would appreciate you sentencing all eleven of the defendants at one time, since they were all charged with the same crimes." The wish was granted, but six defendants still had not arrived. The Judge called for a fifteen-minute recess. Ten minutes into the recess, Thomas came in, out of breath, and went straight to the front of the courtroom to tell Granddaddy they had arrived. Thomas was told to bring in the six remaining defendants to sit by him. He was to peep through the door and watch for Granddaddy to stand, which would be the signal discussed previously, to bring in the wives and children. The Judge returned to the bench and called the court to order.

"Will all of the defendants please stand and approach the bench."

As the defendants rose, so did Granddaddy. This gesture activated the signal previously given to Thomas to bring in the wives and children and seat them behind Granddaddy.

The doors to the courtroom swung open and you have never seen such a sight, much less in a federal courtroom. The women were all wearing torn and ragged clothes; each holding from one to two babies in each arm. They were followed by four to seven kids, all coughing, noses running and the worst-looking, worn-out clothing that could be worn without falling off. All were barefooted and did just what they had been instructed to do: cry, cough, and blow their noses.

Thomas led them down the aisle to the three rows of benches behind Granddaddy. The Judge was shocked at such a sight, but had a good idea of what was going on.

All eleven defendants faced the Judge and were asked if they had anything to say. As the judge went from defendant one to defendant number eleven, all repeated the same words they had been instructed to say. "Judge, can I ask my family to stand so you can see how badly I'm needed at home?"

This was done, as the Judge went down the line, calling each defendant by name. The coughing, nose blowing and crying almost covered the voice of the Judge. The Judge called for a short recess, and asked Granddaddy if he would approach the bench.

"Damn you, Dick, you have beat me this time, but don't ever appear in my courtroom again."

Granddaddy only said, "Judge, how are you going to take care of this crowd of women and children if you send their fathers to the pen for three years?"

At this, Granddaddy returned to his seat without the aid of his walking stick. The court was called back into session. The Judge screamed out the sentences over the crying, coughing, and nose blowing of the children. As the Judge read each name, each defendant said, "Yes sir," and waited for the sentence.

"I sentence each of you to three years in the federal pen with the time to be served while you are on probation. Go back to your families and don't let me see you again. As for you, Captain Dick, see that the whole crowd gets back to the plantation; don't leave any of them here. We can hardly take care of our own."

Granddaddy stood and said, "Thank you, Judge," and in the same breath invited him to Finchburg for a spring turkey hunt.

The crowd returned to Finchburg, the crops were planted, and the defendants were very careful . . . at least for the next three years.

Botank and Liza Williams. Botank was one of the best moonshine makers on the plantation.

12

Why There's No Oil in Finchburg

ONE cool November afternoon a stranger drove up to the store, introduced himself to Granddaddy, and asked his permission to walk over his land. He was representing an oil company, and they were interested in leasing land. Granddaddy gave his permission, and the stranger left, going down the road toward the river. Later that afternoon, the stranger came back and approached Granddaddy for permission to hunt. He said he had never seen such beautiful woods and such an abundance of game.

Granddaddy said, "Sure, just help yourself and feel at home."

"Captain Dick, how will I keep from getting lost?" the stranger said.

"That's easy. Just park at the foot of the long hill, go to the branch and follow it down to the swamp. It will lead you right back to where you started."

The next morning the stranger was on the bank of the branch by daylight, walking south and shooting squirrels. At dark Granddaddy sent Thomas to the swamp to see if he was all right. His car was there, but the oilman was not to be found. Thomas, thinking the man had returned another way, returned to the big house where the family was eating supper.

Granddaddy told Thomas that if the oilman had not shown up

by daylight, a search party would go into the swamp to try and locate him. Morning arrived, and a large frost covered the countryside, with the temperature in the low thirties. The oilman's car was checked, but there was still no sight of him. The search party was told by Granddaddy that he had instructed the man to follow the branch and it would lead him back to where he had started, never believing that anyone was that dumb.

This gave Thomas, the leader, a start because he knew the branch went south through the swamp and five miles downstream before it ran into Flat Creek. It was easy to lose sight of the branch due to old ponds and sloughs throughout the swamp. Two miles below where the car was parked, a torn piece of shirt was found hanging from a thick clump of bamboo briars. Nearby were two spent shotgun shells, with deep footprints in the mud. Also, behind the man's footprints a running wild hog made several distinct tracks. This was the first clue as to the direction the oilman was traveling.

After the encounter with the wild hog, no more tracks were seen near the branch. Later that afternoon, near a thicket on the banks of Flat Creek, five miles from his car, he was found, clothes in rags, bleeding and crying like a baby. No gun could be found, and he had no idea where it was. The search party took turns helping him walk toward his car. Thomas drove the oilman and his car back to the store. Granddaddy insisted on him getting into some dry clothes, but all he would say was, "No, thank you, I have to be going."

We were never worried with the oilman wanting to hunt again; in fact, we never saw him again.

I have always wondered if this is the reason that we do not have oil wells at Finchburg today.

13

The Great Fall Turkey Hunt

DECEMBER was here, and with it came the coldest spell of the year. Every year, two weeks before Christmas, a good friend of Granddaddy's, who happened to be looked upon as the most famous doctor in Mobile, came to Finchburg to turkey hunt. Granddaddy was always his guide, because the doctor could not call turkeys, and he felt more comfortable with someone that knew the swamp. The first two days they killed only two young gobblers, but the doctor wanted to kill an old gobbler.

The old swamp ponds and sloughs were frozen with a thin coat of ice. On the afternoon of the second day, a large group of turkeys were flushed, and they scattered across a frozen pond. Granddaddy told the doctor they needed to ease out without disturbing them anymore, and return to the same spot before day the next morning.

After eating one of Sara Lee's breakfasts consisting of biscuits, eggs, sausage, ham, grits, jams, and fried salt-mackerel, they were ready for the woods. The temperature was nineteen degrees and continually dropping. The clouds were heavy, and it appeared a winter storm was moving in. Sleet began to fall on the pickup's windshield, as the two hunters headed toward the deep swamp. Bad weather had never been a barrier for a turkey hunter, and this morning was no exception. It was 4:15 a.m., when they parked the truck and started walking toward the old pond where the turkeys were roosting. The walk took fifteen minutes, and the sleet had begun falling much harder.

At last they reached the edge of the frozen pond. The wind was blowing slightly but seemed to calm as daylight approached. Granddaddy found a huge, downed white oak tree that had blown over, lying parallel to the pond. It made a perfect blind, plus added some protection from the sleet falling on their faces. They were laying behind the log, which was on the opposite edge of the pond.

Daylight was approaching. Wood ducks filled the air with their whistling sounds and could be heard all over the swamp. The ducks were headed for a running stream or pond which was not frozen, so they could feed on the water oak acorns. Some mallards were heard, but most were wood ducks. Just at daylight several yelps came from different turkeys roosting over the pond in front of the hunters. A better spot could not have been found for the hunters. Granddaddy always yelped with a large homemade cedar box that is very similar to the Lynch Box that we know today.

Two clucks and three very low yelps created a racket, which sounded like there were turkeys in every tree. Several deep yelps seemed to indicate the sound of old gobblers coming from several directions. Most turkey hunters know old gobblers will not mix with younger turkeys. They prefer to stay in groups of two to ten of their own age. In the fall and winter, this group of turkeys was mixed with young gobblers, hens and older gobblers. Granddaddy whispered to the doctor that at least two old gobblers were roosted to his left. A hen cackled, and the turkeys flew over their heads going in all directions, and landed within gunshot range behind them. Granddaddy slowly peeked around to see if any old turkeys were in the flock. He whispered to the doctor that they were young turkeys and the older turkeys were still on the roost.

About that time, three old gobblers flew down on the opposite side of the pond from the hunters, just out of gun range. Stretching their wings, they began to walk away from the swamp pond on the opposite side from the hunters. They were moving west toward the riverbank. The sleet and rain started to pick up, but not loud enough to drown out the scratching and other noises made by the young turkeys, which were still in gun range behind them.

Granddaddy made several loud yelps toward the old gobblers. Two answered but did not seem to want to come their way. Soon the bunch of young turkeys fed off, heading further away from the pond and hunters. It was so cold that both hunters were shaking. The wind suddenly calmed for a few minutes, so Granddaddy made several more loud yelps. Just as he finished, an older gobbler with his beard swinging like a black rope came to within fifty steps of the edge of the pond. Granddaddy told the doctor to get ready and be very still. The old gobbler was huge and was a beautiful sight, walking toward the hunters at his own pace.

What seemed like an hour, but was only five minutes, brought the old gobbler in gun range, just across the pond. Granddaddy told the doctor to take good aim and fire. At the sound of the gun, the turkey fell back and began flopping. Just behind the dying turkey, two more turkeys could be heard flying away toward the swamp. All three turkeys had been coming toward them, with this one in the lead. The other two could not be seen. Granddaddy congratulated the doctor and told him to go get the turkey, so they could get out of the sleet and go home to a warm fire. The doctor looked at Granddaddy and asked how far it was around the end of the pond.

Granddaddy acted as if he was not sure, and said, "It's at least three miles to the end. I hate to see you walk that far in this cold and sleet and you may get lost. I can't go with you because of my arthritis. I suggest you take off your clothes and quickly wade over to the other side to get the turkey. It's not far and you won't have time to get cold."

The doctor hesitated, but finally decided to strip and wade across the pond. What Granddaddy did not tell him was . . . the pond had a deep run in the middle and the water would surely be over his head.

The doctor, with only his hat on, started wading out across the pond. In the meantime, Granddaddy walked a hundred yards beyond a treetop located around the upper end of the lake and waited for the doctor to step off into the deep part. Out came a blood-screaming yell, and the doctor hollered, "That damn thing is deep!"

He swam and waded over to the other side, shaking like an old, cold wet dog. He reached down and picked up the huge gobbler, not noticing Granddaddy standing next to him, dry as he could be.

"Doctor, that is a fine bird," said Granddaddy.

"How in the hell did you get here without getting wet?" sputtered the doctor.

Granddaddy apologized and said, "Doctor, I didn't realize the upper end of this pond was so close. I just walked around it, and by then you were already near the bank. By the way, where is your hat?"

The doctor looked straight at Granddaddy and said, "You better not tell this in Mobile or anywhere else!"

They walked around the pond and retrieved the doctor's clothes. As they returned to the truck, Granddaddy said, "That sure is a fine bird."

The doctor replied, "Go to hell!"

14

High Brass Shells

GRANDDADDY loved to eat ducks, so one cold freezing day he sent for Alma to come to the store. The weather was half-sleeting and half-snowing. Alma got on his old mule and headed for the store, which was a good three miles away. In the winter, Granddaddy and several others were always sitting by the warm potbellied stove in the middle of the store. Alma entered the store with his thick horn-rimmed glasses fogging up from the heat of the stove. He was freezing, and his clothes were heavy with snow and sleet. Granddaddy invited Alma to join them by the stove, and he gladly accepted the invitation.

Alma was anxious to find out what Granddaddy wanted, but waited for him to bring up the subject. The time was 10 a.m., and the snow and sleet was getting worse, with the temperature dropping fast.

Granddaddy said to Alma, "Thomas just came back from the lower swamp pond, and it's full of ducks. I want you to take these shells and I'll give you a dime a duck, if you bring them back to me before dark. These are new shells and will kill a long way off, so see how many you can get before the pond freezes over. Tomorrow will be too late, because the radio said the high for tomorrow would only be twelve degrees."

Alma left in a hurry, with the new box of shells and a hurried-up mule. Alma stopped at his house to get a croaker sack and his old double-barreled rabbit-eared shotgun. He told Arlean, his wife, where he was going and hoped to be back soon.

Arlean did not mind Alma going off for the day because she could go into the smokehouse and steal Alma's whiskey. This was all right because she loved a drink better than most men did. Alma never figured out what was going on with his whiskey. He did not drink and did not know that Arlean did. Arlean would pour herself a half-gallon and then refill the gallon jug with water. Alma always wondered why his whiskey was not as strong as it should be. It seemed his customers were always complaining.

As Alma left, Arlean yelled, "Bring me back a coon if you see one."

With his thick glasses, Alma could spot a coon better than anyone on the plantation. Hackberry trees grew along the trail bordering the swamp. Alma spotted a coon eating hackberries not too high in one of the trees. He had several shells in his pocket that belonged to him, so he used one of these shells to kill the coon. It was a big fat boar coon, and he knew Arlean would be pleased.

Alma and the old mule approached the swamp pond. It sounded like every duck in the country was squealing, quacking, and splashing all over the lake. They were eating the abundance of acorns which had fallen into the pond from the overhanging water oaks. Alma hitched the mule and got his gun and sack, along with the new box of shells, and walked toward the pond. The air filled with rising ducks, but Alma never raised his gun, because he had a better plan to take more ducks with fewer shots.

A small narrow ridge of dry land protruded toward the center of the lake, and near the end was an old half-rotten stump. Alma crawled up behind the old stump, which made a perfect blind. He opened the new box of shells and loaded both barrels of the old double barrel. He had never seen any shells like these. They were blue and had brass halfway up the shells. What Alma did not know was they were the new high-powered number four shots with three grams of powder, made by Peters. Alma could not read, so the numbers did not make any difference. All the shells he had ever shot were very low brass and did not kick much. The plan that Alma had was to wait awhile hidden behind the stump, and let a flock of ducks swim close enough for a shot. He would then discharge both barrels at them at once. The ducks that Alma had flushed were circling and landing back on the lake with more new ducks arriving. Alma was so excited about his plan that he did not notice the sleet had increased and the edges around the pond were turning to ice. The ducks were feeding and beating their wings to keep the pond from freezing, all the time getting closer to Alma's hiding place. Very soon, a large flock of ducks was in range. Alma would always whistle just before shooting in order that the ducks raise their heads. Taking careful aim and with a loud whistle, he fired both barrels.

This is all Alma remembered for a long time. When he did come to, his glasses were hanging from both ears, broken in the center. Blood was running from his nose; he was flat on his back with the fore piece of the gun in one hand, the stock in the other hand, and gosh knows which way the barrels went. His hat was floating, along with eleven dead ducks. Those high-powered shells had completely destroyed a double barrel, a pair of glasses, and caused a bleeding nose and a shoulder that was blue all over. Alma gathered up the pieces of his gun, his hat, and the eleven ducks and set out for the store, with his glasses still hanging from each ear.

Alma could hardly see from the blood and his broken glasses, but the old mule knew the way to the store and delivered Alma to the front porch. Thomas left the stove and went to the porch to see what the commotion was about. Alma was coming through the door dragging the sack of ducks and pieces of his gun in one hand and the box of shells in the other. He went straight to Granddaddy, gave him the shells, and told him he never wanted to see another high brass shell.

Granddaddy asked what was wrong and Alma replied, "Them shells kill on both ends." Alma got a new pair of glasses, a new single-barrel gun, and two dollars for the ducks, but up until his death you could not give him a high-brass shell.

This is what Alma dumped on the front porch of the big store after duck hunting for granddaddy. An old gun in three pieces, a pair of broken eye-glasses, a croker sack splattered with blood from Alma's nose, eleven ducks, and the remains of a box of high brass shells.

15

Murry and the Knot Hole

MURRY was Uncle Fonde's fox hunting buddy and loved the sport. Murry had names for the various wild birds and animals. The one I remember was the name he had given the old hoot owl. He called him Jessie. Murry would be in the woods fox hunting at night, and the owls could be heard hooting from all directions. His favorite words were, "There's old Jessie."

Murry had a bad habit of reaching his hand into every hole or hollow that he found in the trees all over the woods. One day T. B., Doe, and I were squirrel hunting. Murry never carried a gun but enjoyed following us. On this day, we were hunting in the hills, where more holes and hollows were found closer to the ground in many of the trees.

Murry located a nice round hole in a beech tree. The hole was a little too high for Murry to reach from the ground, so by skinning up the tree several feet Murry was able to reach into the hole. All of a sudden, all hell broke loose. Murry was yelling that something in the hole was squealing and flopping. Running toward the tree, we asked Murry what was going on. All he would say was, "Murry has got Jessie and Jessie has got Murry."

After tugging for several minutes, Old Jessie and Murry's hand

86

popped out of the hole. Old Jessie had buried his claws deep into Murry's hand and blood was flying from the claw punctures in his hand. The owl freed himself and flew away, leaving Murry wounded.

From that day forward, whenever an owl hooted, Murry would always say, "There's old Jessie." Murry learned his lesson from this experience, and never again did he stick his hand into a hollow or hole.

16

The Coon Dogs Treed a Haint

MANZIE was our main coon-hunting guide. On week nights, he would stay in the woods all night or until we were ready to go home. On Saturday nights, midnight signaled the end of the hunt. Manzie always said, "If you hunt after midnight on Saturday, when the Lord's Day started, the Lord will send all kinds of 'haints' after you."

Someone gave me two plastic blow-up black monkeys, with large shiny eyes, made from some kind of bright glass that reflected in the dark. When you blew air into the plastic monkeys, their tails and legs were made to hook onto tree limbs. This particular Saturday afternoon, Doe, T. B., and I begged Granddaddy for the use of his truck, so that before the night hunt started, we could look for coon tracks down on the swamp road.

He finally consented, provided we would agree to bring back some lightwood. This was a deal, because it would not take us long to gather a pickup full of lightwood with little effort. We had planned to have some fun with those plastic monkeys by crawling up a tree and placing them on two limbs, one on one side of the tree and one on the other.

We drove down the old dirt road past Manzie's house, not stopping until we reached the bottom of the hill on the outskirts of the river bottom swamp. Next to the road was a large water oak still full of leaves. The tree was easy to climb with its many branches, so T. B. scaled up the tree with both monkeys in his pockets. About twenty feet up the tree; T. B. inflated one of the monkeys and placed him as far as he could reach out on a limb. The plastic legs and tail were ideal for attaching the monkey to the limb. T. B. went higher in the tree and placed the second monkey on a limb on the opposite side of the tree. Even in daylight, those glass eyes were shining. Those monkeys were the worst-looking animals we had ever seen in a tree.

With our mission accomplished, we headed back to the store. With a quick stop at Manzie's house we let him know we would pick him and the dogs up at dark. The plan was to hunt until close to midnight and just before arriving at the truck, we would shine the eyes of the monkeys in the oak tree and try to shoot them out. We could not wait until dark. When dark arrived, Doe, T. B., and I got into the old pickup and headed straight to Manzie's house. Manzie was waiting with all the dogs tied to the front porch. The dogs numbered at least twelve, with no thoroughbred in the whole bunch. The pack was made up of bulldogs, hounds, and some other unknown bloodlines. Manzie's main dog went by the name of Headman. Manzie gave him this name because he always led the pack. All of the dogs, except Headman, were thrown into the pickup body. Manzie would always hold Headman in his lap.

We picked up another coon hunter by the name of Nig, who was already half drunk, but ready to go with us. We stopped the pickup just above the oak tree that held the monkeys.

Dogs, boys and men unloaded, and we boys made it a point not to even look toward the big oak as we passed by. Just as we approached the swamp, Old Headman let out a series of barks, and the race was on. After thirty minutes, they treed in a tall oak. We easily found the coon and added him to our bag with one shot. The next coon was not as easy, because he chose to run in and out of an old swamp pond. This race lasted for two hours before the dogs finally treed him in a large tupelo gum out in the pond.

Wading about boot-top high through the pond, we finally arrived at the tree. Old Headman was raring up on the tree, barking with every breath. We soon located the coon and added another to the bag. We were a long way from the truck, and the time was fast approaching midnight, so we started out. We all carried flashlights, but I carried the largest light.

Manzie had two dogs that had a habit of treeing if you shined a light up the tree, regardless of whether or not a coon was in the tree. Before we got to the pickup, Manzie kept mumbling that he was not going to hunt after midnight even if the dogs did tree.

Manzie led the group. T. B., Doe, and I could not wait until we got to the oak tree. Manzie and the dogs went right by the tree and were almost to the truck when I shined the large light up the oak tree. The monkey's eyes were as big as silver dollars, and a bright red and yellow reflection came from them. The eyes looked almost as large as the jet-black bodies of the animals, both of which could easily be seen by the light of a full moon. The two dogs that loved to tree up any tree with a light shining in it were already under the tree barking at the tops of their voices. We waited until drunken Nig caught up with us before showing him the large eyes in the tree.

Nig hollered, "Lord, Br'er Manzie, come here and look what a coon. I ain't never seen no coon with eyes that bright and black."

Manzie did not want to come down to the tree because he was sure it was after midnight and was now Sunday morning. T. B., Doe, and I added to Manzie's curiosity by commenting on what a large black coon it was, with the biggest eyes that we had ever seen. Manzie could not stand it anymore, so he brought the gun back to the tree. I waited until he got to the tree and shined the light toward the bright eyes. Manzie said, "I ain't never seen no coon as black and with them kind of eyes before."

We let Manzie have the first shot. With careful aim, he fired; nothing but leaves and small limbs fell. The large hand moved and the eyes were still shining as brightly as ever. After six shots, the animal did not move. Manzie didn't understand why the coon didn't fall nor at least turn his head. Manzie asked, "What time it is?"

I looked at my watch and told him it was 1 a.m. Manzie started walking away, saying, "The Good Lord done put a haint in that tree. Let's go home now!"

Just then I walked to the other side of the tree and flashed the light back up the tree. T. B. hollered, "Thar's another coon, just as big as the other, with the same kind of eyes."

We begged Manzie to bring the gun and shells. The same thing happened with this "coon."

The last four of our shells were used, and still both animals remained in the tree.

Nig, stumbling around in his drunken stupor said, "Us coming back tomorrow and get them coons."

Manzie said, "Br'er Nig, them ain't no coons. Them is haints that the Lord done put down here cause we is hunting on Sunday."

T. B., Doe, and I were biting our lips to keep from laughing.

We never told Manzie the truth, and Nig was too drunk to remember anything.

17

A Day of Fishing on Mill Creek

T. B. and I talked Edna into taking us fishing on Mill Creek, which was three miles from Edna's house and was a great creek for bluegill and bass. It did not take much persuading to get Edna ready to go, because she loved fishing as much as we did. She was afraid to go by herself, and we were not allowed to go unless she was with us. This made it a good deal for all of us. Mill Creek was a small stream that had been dammed up by beavers. This had created a series of smaller lakes that ran for two miles up and down the creek. In these lakes we found some of the best bluegill and bass anywhere in the surrounding area. We would walk from one dam to the other, catching fish wherever we stopped.

T. B. and I wanted to beat Edna fishing on this day, so we decided to go to the last dam, just before Mill Creek emptied into Flat Creek. Flat Creek was affected by the rise and fall of the river and was backed up by a recent rise in the river. This resulted in an overflowing of the dam in Mill Creek, which spread out some thirty yards from the original creek bed. The overflow water was from ankle deep to knee deep. We decided to wade out to where we could reach the original creek bed.

Just as my line and worm hit the water, a nice bull bluegill was on it. I quickly put him in a sack that was tied around my neck for that purpose. By this time, T. B. had joined me, and he soon added a bluegill to his credit. Between the dry ground and where T. B. and I were fishing, something made a huge splash in the water, sending ripples toward us. Uneasy, but too interested in catching fish, we convinced each other it was only a beaver splashing his tail in the water. After catching several more fish, we had almost forgotten about the disturbance behind us.

At this point T. B. happened to glance over his shoulder toward the huge splash, and without a word, threw down his pole and took off . . . splashing through the water, running like a deer through the pond. Curious as to what was going on, I glanced behind me and saw a huge head leaving a perfect v-shaped wake in the water as it swam toward us. There was no doubt in my mind as to why T. B. took off. A large alligator was heading toward us. Ten yards toward the creek

The results of one of the other days of fishing on Mill Creek.

channel, T. B. had already started up a tree. Before his feet were up too high for me to reach, I made it to the tree and grabbed hold of them. I could not climb the tree, and I made darn sure T. B. was not going to leave me in the water with the gator. I grabbed hold of both of T. B.'s feet, and down the tree he slid. About the same time, the big gator rolled in the water splashing water all over us.

T. B. grabbed me by the seat of my pants, and pushed me up the tree, while scampering up right behind me. We both made it out of danger by only a few seconds. We stayed in the tree for what seemed like two hours, but was actually only several minutes. After waiting for the gator to surface, which he never did, we decided to make a getaway and go for the dry ground.

We made a mad dash down the tree, running, wading and swimming toward the bank. We did not try to retrieve our fishing poles and bait because these were the last things on our minds.

We hustled back to the spot where Edna was, out of breath with no poles and bait and wet all over. We were not about to tell Edna that a big old alligator ran us out of the creek.

She was terribly afraid of snakes and would not even go near a creek where a gator had been seen. We wanted to come back in the future (but not wade out in the backwater). We told Edna that Flat Creek was rising and we had gotten cut off from our poles and had to leave them. I guess she believed us, because we returned to Mill Creek many times and caught a lot of fish.

We never saw that gator again, and we surely did not search for him.

18

An Airplane in the Field

THE year 1943 rolled around, and we were in the middle of some of the worst days of World War II. Daddy and Uncle Maiben were still in service, with Granddaddy and Uncle Fonde left to run the farm. It was time to break the fields and get ready for planting. Uncle Fonde sent Otis, along with the large Farm-All tractor, to break the big field. Just after lunch Uncle Fonde went to check on Otis and see how the plowing was coming along. Neither Otis nor the tractor could be seen, but the faint sound of a tractor could be heard off in the woods.

Uncle Fonde quickly went toward the noise and found a plowed path through the briars, bushes, and trees leading to the tractor. It was stuck on a stump with the wheels spinning and the motor still running. Otis could not be seen anywhere. After calling for several minutes, Uncle Fonde heard Otis holler from the other side of the field. Uncle Fonde switched off the tractor and went to see what had happened to Otis.

Otis had cuts and blood all over his body. His overalls were almost torn from his body. Briars were hanging from his well-torn clothes, and his eyes looked like two white saucers. Before Uncle Fonde had the opportunity to ask what had happened, Otis started telling him. It seems that he was in the middle of the big field, when

The Farm-All tractor that Otis abandoned when the plane surprised him in the field.

he heard a loud roaring and singing sound behind him. He looked back and saw a huge airplane at ground level, headed straight toward him. He was not about to let that thing hit him, so he jumped from the tractor and headed for the woods. The tractor chugged on into the woods on one side of the field, while Otis went out the other side.

Uncle Fonde found Otis's tale hard-to-believe, but several days later all of the newspapers told of airplanes diving at objects all along the river from Claiborne to Selma. Most of the objects were tractors and their drivers, who were working in the big fields along the riverbanks. It seems the United States had sent a squadron of French pilots to Craig Field in Selma to train them in our most advanced fighter, the P-40, which was noted for its speed. The Claiborne Bridge was the turning point on their training mission, before the return trip back upriver to Craig Field.

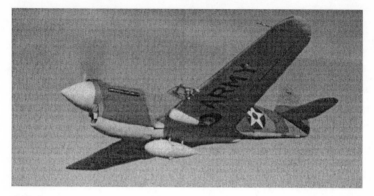

A P-40.

The pilots, who were looking for excitement, made strafing passes at the tractors just to have fun. Before this practice was brought to the attention of the commanding officer at Craig Field, many mules, wagon drivers, and tractor drivers ended up in the woods scared to death.

From that day on, Otis always stopped the tractor and cut the engine when he heard an airplane flying low.

19

A Bed of Wild Pigs

ONE cold night in December, Nig decided to go deep into the lower swamp and do some coon hunting. Unable to find anyone to go with him, he took several drinks of his favorite liquor and filled a quart jar to take on the hunt. The following is the story Nig repeated to us later:

His three dogs went deep into the swamp before barking on a coon track. After several hours of treeing, swimming, and re-treeing throughout the old sloughs and ponds, the dogs remained under one tree. Firing up a lightwood torch so he could see, he started toward the dogs. As Nig struggled through a thicket of briars, vines and palmetto bushes he stepped into the middle of a bed of wild pigs.

The pigs squealed, and the old sow could be heard, with her teeth snapping, crashing through the thicket toward him, making all kinds of sounds, none of which were friendly. Nig remembered running with all the speed he could generate. The burning torch was thrown away, as he raced through the dark swamp with the sow in hot pursuit. This was all he remembered until the next day when the sun was setting.

His head was killing him when he came to and dried blood was caked all over his face. He was finally coming to his senses as he lay under a huge white oak tree. The bark was almost slick, just at head level on the tree. He had centered the trunk of the tree and knocked himself out. With the moonshine still in his system and the force of the lick, he did not come to before the sun started setting on the following afternoon.

For several days afterwards, Nig had dizzy spells and one heck of a headache.

Left, Nig (in overalls) talking to someone in town. Above, a wild pig, minding its own business.

20

Hog Dogs from Washington

FRANK Boykin, a Democrat from Mobile, was our Congressman in Washington. He was a good friend of Granddaddy's, both socially and politically, or at least he pretended to be. Each Christmas, Representative Boykin would send Granddaddy a prize hunting dog, or at least he said it was prized. The dogs were always registered, with the papers being processed and put on file. The files would always be late arriving.

Granddaddy found out some way that Frank was getting these high-priced dogs, from the animal shelter in Washington, D.C. His only expense was the transportation from the pound in Washington to Finchburg, Alabama. Transportation in those days was in the five-to ten-dollar range. Most of the dogs Boykin sent over the years would not even run for a biscuit, and did not even know what hunting was about.

One particular Christmas, Granddaddy made the mistake of remarking, in the presence of Frank and several friends from Mobile, that the wild hogs were taking over the plantation and were a danger to the hands working in the fields. It was not long after this just two days before Christmas, the L & N railroad agent, notified Granddaddy that two bulldogs had arrived on the afternoon train. The Agent happened to be my Uncle Jessie Carter, on my mother's side of the family. The label on the crate was written in large letters: PLEASE NOTIFY R. B. WILLIAMS, SR., THAT TWO HUNTING HOG DOGS, THE BEST AVAILABLE WITH REGISTERED PAPERS BEING PROCESSED, ARE COMPLIMENTS FROM FRANK BOYKIN, DEMOCRATIC REPRESENTATIVE FROM ALABAMA.

Uncle Jessie delivered the dogs to Granddaddy's house on West Claiborne Street in Monroeville where Aunt Julia and Aunt Louise lived. When the dogs arrived, they had no idea what to do with them. All they could do was feed and water them for the night, until Thomas arrived the next morning to take the dogs to the plantation. There the dogs could start eliminating some of the overpopulated wild hogs. The dogs were a mixed breed, one part Boxer, with white spots on red, indicating that the mother did not notice nor care about the bloodline of the father. The other dog had all of the markings of a full-blooded bulldog, white in color, and with a mean look on his face.

Representative Frank Boykin.

Thomas delivered the dogs to the plantation, and Granddaddy was anxious to see just what Frank had sent him. However, from the past history of the dogs that had been presented as gifts from Representative Boykin, Granddaddy had little faith in the ability of these dogs to hunt.

Most of the wild hogs were located in the upper range of the plantation, known as the Upper Swamp, which was in the charge of Robert Boykin, the overseer. Anxious to test the ability of these high-priced hunting dogs from Washington, D.C., supposedly skilled in catching wild hogs, according to Representative Frank Boykin's description, Granddaddy arranged with Robert to supervise a wild hog hunt.

Granddaddy invited several of his friends, including one lawyer, to join in the wild hog hunt. One politician was invited, but he, after learning the source of the new hunting dogs, declined the invitation.

The hunt was scheduled for Friday morning after Christmas. The weather was down in the teens, but no sleet or rain was forecast. Everyone was looking forward to the hunt. After a predawn break-fast, the hunters were "foaming at the bit" to test the new hunting dogs.

The journey from the big house to the upper swamp was only thirty minutes, depending on the mode of transportation. This particular morning the transportation was motorized vehicles.

Gents Edwards, incidentally one of the top makers of white lightning in the entire area of Finchburg, lived two hundred yards up the dirt road from Robert Boykin's house. Gents always kept a yard full of chickens, from laying hens to pullets. The chickens had a free range around the house with no fences, and often wandered into the surrounding woods to feed. Gents also kept several goats around the house to go and come as they pleased. Robert Boykin kept several hogs in a pen behind his house, including an old sow with a litter of young pigs.

The hunters, along with Thomas and the new hunting dogs,

arrived at Robert's house just as daylight was breaking. Robert lived at the top of a long hill overlooking the Alabama River swamp. The hill could be treacherous, especially during wet weather. The hill was a half-mile long with a steep valley on one side and very little room for traveling on the other side. Robert and Thomas decided to tie the two dogs and walk them to the swamp, down the steep hill. The hunters who were brave enough to drive down the hill were told to meet the dog handlers at the foot of the hill. Some hunters drove, but most decided to walk after viewing the steep hill. When the dog handlers and hunters arrived at the foot of the hill, it was decided by Robert and Thomas to look for fresh hog tracks before turning the dogs loose. It was not long before fresh wild hog signs were sighted. The mixed breed boxer with red and white spots was turned loose first. The dog never stopped to smell the first hog track, but ran back up the steep hill toward Robert's house. The white bulldog was turned loose and soon disappeared into the woods, never making a

Robert Boykin with mule.

sound for at least two hours. The dog handlers and hunters were very much upset because of the poor performance of these supposedly great hunting dogs.

The sun had started to rise, but the temperature was still below freezing. A large open fire was built, and all of the hunters were soon surrounding the warm blaze. The wild hog hunt, at this particular time, was put on hold. The hunters were beginning to feel the warmth of the huge fire of piled-up logs and fat lightwood stumps and were starting to ask questions about when the hunt would get underway. Just about then, Gents Edwards could be seen coming down the steep hill with a mule and wagon. In the center of the wagon bed was a five-gallon, charred wooden barrel, surrounded by a thick layer of sawdust with many fruit jars embedded in the sawdust.

Robert and Thomas hurried to join Gents at the wagon to get a drink. After they drank, they asked the hunters if they would also like a drink of fresh cool spring water. Most of the hunters had warmed up and decided to get a cool drink of spring water, to keep from hurting the feelings of their hosts, namely Thomas, Robert, and Gents. What the hunters did not know was that the cool spring water was one hundred percent "shinny" (white lightning). The so-called spring water was strong to the taste, but after swallowing it gave the participant a feeling of warmth over the entire body. The warm feeling offset the strong burning sensation that occurred when first swallowed, especially since the temperature was in the teens and anything warm felt good.

A vehicle was heard, at this time, coming down the steep hill. Doe was at the steering wheel and Granddaddy sat in the right front seat. Granddaddy got out of the vehicle and called Gents over to the side of the truck, out of hearing from the hunters. Gents was told he was needed at home right away. Hurrying up the hill, Gents could not imagine what could be wrong. Arriving in his yard, he could not help noticing chicken feathers and dead chickens all around his house. Gents's wife met him at the front door, all excited and started relating the story of what had been going on. According to Gents's wife, a mixed-breed dog with white and red spots came up the road from Robert's house and started catching and killing chickens. The last time she saw the dog, he was chasing the last old rooster into the woods. From that day on, we never saw or heard from that hunting dog again. It took Gents almost a year to rebuild his flock of chickens and several weeks to locate his goats.

Meanwhile, after an hour of sipping spring water, the hunters were talking louder, laughing, and telling old hunting stories of the past. The hog hunt was almost forgotten by everyone except Robert and Thomas. They left the crowd and went up the hill to Robert's house to find out what had happened to the hunting dogs. Annie, Robert's wife, met them in the front yard. She told of the red and white spotted dog going up the road toward Gents's house and the sound of chickens being attacked from all directions. She also told Robert the white bulldog had tried to enter the pen with the old sow and pigs, barking and growling as if he was going to catch every hog in the pen. The last time she saw the dog, the old sow was chasing the bulldog across the yard toward the crib. The dog scooted under the crib, and the only thing that saved the dog was the old sow was too large to get under the crib. Robert and Thomas went back under the hill and called Granddaddy away from the crowd and related to him what had happened with the "hog dogs."

Granddaddy walked over to the hunters and told them that both hunting dogs were running a huge black, wild boar that had just run through Robert's backyard, and the last time they were heard barking, they were heading toward the river. The hunters were in good spirits and decided they had enough of hog hunting for the day. Most started home, but some went by the wagon with the spring water, to get a fruit jar full to take home with them.

All the hunters expressed to Granddaddy how much they had enjoyed the hog hunt. Granddaddy apologized to the hunters for not catching the first wild hog, but made the statement that some highly bred hog dogs would run for miles before catching a hog. Granddaddy promised several of the hunters a puppy from the first litter that the spotted female would deliver after breeding with the white bulldog. Several of the hunters were anxious to receive such a valuable gift, especially the hunters that had participated in drinking two fruit jars of Gents's spring water.

21

The Big Bad Bull

GRANDDADDY had a huge Hereford bull in the pasture behind the barn. The bull hated everyone, especially Doe, T. B., and me. It would run at us every time we got near him. I had received a B.B. gun from Santa Claus that Christmas, a Daisy Pump, the elite of B.B. guns in those days. I shot at all kinds of targets every day and became a fairly good shot.

In the back pasture, there was a huge mimosa tree that was easy to climb. The old bull had a path he traveled each day that was very close to this tree. For once and all, we were going to get even with this bull. Doe, T. B., and I climbed up into the mimosa tree with my famous B.B. gun. We did not have to wait long before the old bull and a group of cows came down the hill, heading straight for us. We noticed the old bull's penis (that's not what we called it, but we will use the scientific name for now) was hanging down, pink, long, and hard-looking, swaying back and forth under the rear of his stomach and almost in the center of his back legs.

T. B. said, "Shoot that thing hanging down."

Doe added, "I bet he won't run us anymore if you can hit it."

The old bull came closer to the tree as he followed close behind one of the cows in which he was showing particular interest. I took careful aim and fired. That old bull jumped straight up, started

The big bad bull.

turning around and around in circles, and bellowing for dear life. I must have hit the target, because a knot started swelling halfway up his penis. He rolled over and over, and the last time we saw him, he was running for the barn. We slid out of the tree and ran with all our might in the opposite direction.

Doe said, "You reckon' we done killed the bull?"

T. B. added that he "shore" acted like he was dying, and we all imagined the worse. Late that afternoon, we arrived at the store from the opposite side of the road, across from the barn and pasture. Granddaddy wanted to know where we had been. We quickly told him we had been hunting for birds in the old pond behind the store. We had three ricebirds and two baby doves, which we later learned were rose doves. They all looked like small young doves. The old ditch leading from the pond was always full of them in the winter.

Thomas came puffing in the front door, heading straight for Granddaddy. We knew from the look in his eyes that something bad was wrong. Granddaddy asked Thomas, "What in the world is the matter?"

Thomas said, "Captain Dick, something done happened to your bull. His privates are all red and swollen, with a huge knot on it. All he will do is bellow, turn around and around, and fall over rolling on the ground."

Granddaddy told Thomas they probably had too many heifers in the pasture with him.

We did not know what that meant, but we were sure not going to stay around and listen to find out. T. B. did not make us feel any better by saying he did not think the bull was going to live. Thomas moved twenty heifers to another pasture, leaving twenty-two with the old bull. After several days, the old bull was normal, and Granddaddy once again said to Thomas that they must have had too many heifers with the bull.

From that day forward, we never crossed that pasture, nor did we get close to that old bull.

B.B. gun used.

22

Dago and the Big Catfish

THE day before the fourth of July, Granddaddy called some of the tenants together, and told them he would like for them to go to the river and try to catch enough catfish for a large fish fry for the plantation. He suggested they use throw-lines to catch the fish. He sent Thomas, Alma, Nig, Pewee, Eddie, and Dago, who could not swim, but loved to fish.

Granddaddy sent Thomas with the truck to pick up the others and take them to the river. Bait was gathered, and each man had at least two throw-lines. Arriving at the river early that morning, they scattered up and down the river, baiting their hooks and throwing the lines into the river. The July sun was bearing down, so the fishermen retreated up the steep riverbank to seek shade and to wait for the fish to bite. Almost all the fishermen anchored the ends of their lines into bushy limbs that were growing deep into the riverbank at the water's edge. When a fish was hooked, the bush started shaking and could easily be seen by the movement of the trees on the top of the riverbank.

Alma was the best throw-line fisherman in the crowd. He would always attach cowbells to his lines. When a fish was on the hook, the bell would ring, which was especially good at night since the line was hard to see when it was dark.

Several fish were landed before Dago started hollering for help. He had hooked something that he could not handle, and the tight line was about to pull him into the river. Remembering that Dago could not swim, they all yelled for him to let the line and fish go, until they could wear the fish down. This Dago did. Meanwhile, the line was still going up and down in the river, with the limb still attached to the end of the line, bent over into the water. By the time Thomas arrived to help Dago, the huge fish had wrapped the line around and under a willow treetop. This tree had fallen out into the river, but was still attached to the bank by its roots, which kept it from floating away. The limbs at the end of the tree were shaking back and forth as the hooked and tangled fish was trying to get away.

Thomas and Dago pulled with all their strength on the line, thinking they could break the limb and retrieve the fish. This did not happen. The limb held, and the fish would make a run, and the top would give, but not break.

At times the huge catfish would surface, and its size was unbelievable. This was the largest catfish they had ever caught or seen. Dago wanted that fish, but he knew the only way possible to get the fish was to skin the tree and work his way out to the end and break the limb that had the line snagged. Although he knew he could not swim, the temptation was still too much, so he took his shoes off and began crawling out onto the fallen willow tree. Everyone on the bank was giving instructions, but no one had volunteered to help. Dago was almost to the end of the tree. The water was really swift and appeared to be very deep, especially to someone that had never learned to swim.

As Dago reached for the limb that held the tangled line, the fish made a big surge, and into the river Dago tumbled. You have never seen such a commotion. Water was going everywhere. Dago was fighting for dear life and hollering for someone to save him. He went under twice and was almost ready to give up when someone from the bank hollered, "Dago, just stand up!" As a last resort he caught a limb and pulled himself to his feet.

The water came only to his knees. Dago was very much relieved but mad as hell with his fishing partners for not telling him the water was so shallow. Thomas and Alma waded out and helped Dago walk to the bank. He was still shaking and mad. He dared any of them to tell Captain Dick, because he knew he would never hear the last of it. All promised not to tell and began to pull the fish in after one of them broke the limb and released the line. They finally got the huge "blue cat" to shore and decided that with this large fish and what they had already caught, this would be more than enough to feed everyone on the plantation.

Dago lived on the side of the road, long before getting to the store, so Thomas let Dago off at his house to get some dry clothes, and then proceeded on to the store. Granddaddy was amazed at the large fish and gave all the fishermen a cold drink, which in those days meant a grape, strawberry, or orange Ne-Hi, or a Royal Crown, and sometimes a Coca-Cola. The cold drink box was usually filled with water about halfway up the side of the standing bottles, with a large block of ice placed in the insulated box to keep the drinks cold. Before the fishermen could finish their cold drinks, up the road came Dago on his old mule. Granddaddy instructed the fishermen to go and clean the tub of fish for tomorrow's fish fry, and then he motioned for Dago to come and get a cold drink. Dago finished his cold drink and started out to help clean the fish. As he was leaving Granddaddy hollered to Dago, asking him how deep the river was where he had been fishing. All swore that they had not said a word to Granddaddy about the drowning that had almost taken place, but Dago knew better and could never live it down from that day on.

23

The Worst Thing We Ever Treed

MANZIE, T. B., Doe, Papa, and I were coon hunting one cold, dark night. The weather had gone from cold to freezing cold. A thin layer of ice was beginning to form over the mud holes, and we began to wonder if we had on enough clothes. Manzie commented, "Tonight is shore going to be a good night for coon hunting 'cause the moon ain't up, and it is cold." A cold, dark night was always considered the best time for a coon hunt. I could vouch for the statement that it was cold, and I did not see the moon anywhere, so this had to be the perfect night.

Manzie's best dog, Headman, was leading the pack as usual, with Manzie bragging on him with every series of barks. Manzie went so far as to swear that Old Headman would not run anything but a coon at night. It did not take long for the dogs to tree or bay something. We could not tell which, because they were located on the other side of two ridges that had a small steam flowing between them.

As we hurried toward the dogs, Manzie stopped long enough to retrieve several pieces of lightwood and stuck them into the game sack that always hung from his shoulder.

We reached the site where old Headman and the other dogs were barking. They were at the end of a log that was not quite large enough for the dogs to crawl through to get at the coon. Manzie took the lightwood out of his game sack and soon had a huge fire started, which we were all glad to see.

As we were warming up, Papa cut a long green pole, which was long enough to reach through the hollow log. The only problem was the hollow did not go all the way through the log. After careful inspection of the log, Manzie found a small hole in the log, just large enough for the long pole to be inserted, enabling us to push the animal out.

Papa took over the job of ramming the pole into the hole. T. B. took the light and came as close to the opening as his head would allow. T. B. said he could hear the animal scratching. Papa rammed the pole into and down the hollow log. Just as T. B. peeped into the opening of the hollow log, Papa made several hard jabs with the pole and out came the largest "pole cat" that we had ever seen. T. B. fell backwards, and we all ran like the devil in different directions to keep from being sprayed by the "pole cat." However, T. B., Papa, and the dogs were not so lucky, and were well sprayed by the polecat. The scent was unbearable.

The hunt was definitely over at this point. Manzie tied the dogs and let T. B. and Papa lead them home, making sure they were well behind us all the way. I could not resist telling Manzie that he had both a coon and skunk dog in Old Headman.

Manzie replied, "It must have also been a coon in that hollow log, but I ain't going back to see."

24

The Huge Hog Sale

THE swamp was full of wild hogs, most of them descendants of the free-ranging domestic hogs that had become wild over the years. Twice a year Granddaddy sent two crews of tenants into the swamp to trap wild hogs.

A pen was built from saplings and logs. The front of the pen measured five feet wide and the length was at least twenty feet, with a partition, which was a door halfway down the pen. In front of the pen, a sliding door was cut and a long pole attached to the top. The other end of the pole went to the inside of the pen. A short piece of rope was tied to that end of the pole with a short stick attached to the rope. Two stakes were driven into the ground, one on each side of the pole. This was the trigger to the trapdoor. The end of the pole inside the pen was pulled down, lifting the trapdoor. The stick attached to the rope was placed behind the two stakes in the ground. Two ears of corn were attached near the end of the pole, which was near the trigger. With the trap door set, corn was placed in front of the trap and around the pole inside. The hogs would go through the trapdoor eating the corn, bumping into the pole, causing the trigger to slip and let the door fall closed, leaving the hogs trapped.

The traps were set and checked everyday. If the catch was small, the trapped hogs were driven into the back of the pen and the door

The Monroeville Stockyard, site of the huge hog sale.

closed, keeping them from escaping. When a wagonload was cap-
tured, they were tied and taken to a holding pen near the store.
When a truckload was caught, Granddaddy would send them to the
sale in Monroeville.

Now these hogs were not tame, by any means, and would eat
you up if the chance arose. All who knew a wild hog gave them plenty
of respect. A wild hog, if recognized, would not bring one-fourth the
price of a domestic hog at the sale. Granddaddy would mix half a
load of domestic and the other half with wild hogs and send them to
the sale. This worked nicely until Granddaddy decided to send the
entire load of wild hogs by themselves. Sale day came around, and
Thomas loaded the big truck with all wild hogs. You could stick a
limb through the slats on the truck body, and the hogs would bite the
limb in half. That is just how mean and dangerous they were.
Granddaddy and I, along with Doe chauffeuring, headed to
Monroeville stockyard. We wanted to be in the stands when the wild
hogs were driven into the selling arena. The hogs were always sold
before the cow sale began. Three men always worked inside the
arena, using sticks to separate the hogs, so the buyers could look

Jud Jenkins, one of the many Hog buyers standing in front of the pen area at the Monroeville Stockyard.

them over as they were assembled in the pen. The first batch of hogs came through and was sold quickly, bringing a good price.

Mr. Culpepper walked up into the stands and started a conversation with Granddaddy. Mr. Culpepper was the Local County Extension Agent, and was called "Shorty" because he was so tall and lanky. I will never forget the conservation he and Granddaddy had.

Mr. Culpepper said, "Captain Dick, did you bring anything to the sale or are you buying today?"

Granddaddy replied, "Shorty, I believe the two truckloads of hogs that I'm selling today are the best that I have ever raised."

I started laughing under my breath, until Granddaddy tapped me on the leg and I knew to be quiet. Mr. Culpepper told Granddaddy he would try and pass the word that Granddaddy's hogs were a very

Lonnie Everette and Piolet Williams standing in front of the stockyard area.

good batch and to watch out for them. Several minutes passed while Shorty strolled throughout the stands, talking to all the out-of-town buyers.

All of a sudden, all hell broke loose in the back yard, where the hogs were being held in pens, waiting to enter the arena to be auctioned off. Men were running and jumping over the fences, trying to get out of reach of the wild hogs. Someone in the back of the building yelled, "Here comes some of Captain Dick's hogs!"

All three of the men sailed over the fence except Isadore. He was a little too fat to clear the fence. With one leg draped over the fence and the other inside the pen, Isadore was hollering, as the charging hogs came barreling through. Just as a large boar charged toward his leg, one of the helpers pulled him over the fence into another pen. He escaped with only a torn britches leg. Most of the workers had always suspected Captain Dick of mixing his tame hogs with wild hogs, when bringing them to the sale, but after this incident, there was no doubt in their minds. When the cry, "Here comes old man Dick's hogs" was given, everyone hit the fences and gave them the arena.

Mr. Culpepper came up to Granddaddy after the sale and asked what in the world made those hogs so mean. Granddaddy said, "Shorty, those hogs must have gotten scared on the way to the sale. They were real calm when we loaded them."

Shorty
Culpepper,
County
Agent.

25

How Not to Catch a Wild Deer

DURING the early forties, deer had just begun to return to this part of Alabama after being absent for thirty or more years. Overkill and a probable die-off or both were blamed for the scarcity of deer in this area. Mr. Billy Harrigan, who owned Scotch Lumber Company, which was located on the opposite side of the Alabama River, had several deer in a pen. After several years, the herd grew and was turned loose to see if they could make it on their own. They survived, and in a few years they were seen in small numbers on both sides of the river. We were thrilled when we found a track and were really thrilled when we got to see a deer in the wild.

Granddaddy sent Doe and me to check on the pasture fence and see if it was in shape to hold a new load of cows he had just bought. In the front part of the pasture, toward the gate, was an old house-place that was covered over by a thick blanket of kudzu. As we made our way through the thick growth, Doe suddenly stopped just in front of me. There, right in front of us, lying in his bed, was a huge buck deer. Doe whispered that he was going to catch that deer while he was asleep.

Doe, wearing a brand new pair of overalls, jumped straddle the back of the buck, grabbing for his huge rack of horns. The deer and

Doe tore down a half-acre of kudzu. Every now and then I would get a quick look at Doe, as the deer would jump with Doe, hanging on for dear life. Finally the buck jumped the fence, throwing Doe ten feet back into the kudzu. I could not see Doe or the buck for the thick kudzu vines. I yelled at Doe, asking him if he still had a hold on the buck.

Doe answered, "Heck no, and that ain't all. I don't want to see no more deer!"

I made my way through the kudzu to where Doe was lying down, rolling and moaning. Blood was on his arms and legs, and his new overalls were torn to pieces. The deer's hoofs had shredded his clothes just as if someone had cut them all over with a pair of scissors. Doe never tried catching a live deer by jumping on his back again.

Granddaddy, trying not to laugh, said, "Doe, always try to catch a live deer by his back legs."

Two weeks after this incident, Granddaddy sent a crew of three men down into the swamp to cut a load of firewood. Doe went along to drive the truck. Around the edge of the swamp was an old hog wire fence that was used to keep cows and hogs confined, when necessary, because we had open range for both. Just across the fence, twenty yards beyond a briar patch, was an ideal oak tree for making firewood. The crew crossed the fence and started sawing down the oak.

Just as the oak fell across the briar patch, just missing the fence, a doe jumped up from its bed in the patch and ran into the fence. Doe, seeing the opportunity of catching the deer, ran and caught her by her back foot. Doe could not turn the foot loose, because the deer was kicking so fast you could not see Doe's arm or the deer's leg. It was just a blur, with Doe hollering to the top of his lungs. When he did get loose, his arms shook for two days. The deer escaped and another lesson was learned about catching a live deer.

As the deer population continued to grow, more encounters with deer were reported. On the plantation, on the backside of a cornfield, was a small crib, with one door that was used to store unshucked corn. Granddaddy noticed the corn in the crib was growing smaller for some reason. More and more corn went missing every night. The door was found open, and shucks with no corn were always left. Thomas told Granddaddy that he believed one of the tenants was stealing corn and using it for making moonshine.

Thomas and Doe went into action, trying to solve the mystery. They hid and watched the crib half of the night, usually with no results. The next morning the door would be open and more corn would be gone. Thomas and Doe did not know what else to try. Granddaddy suggested they get a cotton basket and fill it halfway with sand and scatter it over the ground near the front door of the crib. "If you all make a good sand bed at the front door, you'll be able to see the tracks in the sand the next morning and we'll be able to tell what we are dealing with."

The sand was spread in front of the crib and leveled off, making it easy to observe any tracks, which might be made. Early next morning, Thomas and Doe hurried to the crib to check the sand bed. Before they reached the crib, they could see the door open and shucks on the ground. Inspection of the sand bed revealed a huge set of deer tracks, leading right up to the crib's front door. The mystery was solved, but the solution was still missing.

Doe would check the crib every time he went near, but could never see the deer with its head in the door eating corn. After several weeks, the deer had eaten all of the corn that could be reached from the outside. The corn continued to disappear, so Doe decided that the old deer was jumping into the crib, eating what he wanted, then leaving. Since the crib had only one door, all he would have to do was slam the door shut, and he would have the thief.

One cold, misty morning Doe started toward the crib. The mist and fog was very thick, and visibility was less than ten yards. The nearer to the crib he got, the more he could hear the noise inside, of shucks being stripped from the corn. The time had arrived; he had finally accomplished the job of getting to the crib with the deer still inside eating. He would be able to approach the door without being detected.

With all of his might, Doe slammed the door shut, and at the same time, all hell broke loose. The noise from inside the crib sounded like the walls of the crib would tear away at any moment. Doe held the door shut as hard as he could. Just as he moved one hand to secure a chain on the door, the deer hit the door with a force that knocked Doe completely out. When he came to his senses, he was under the crib door, flat on the ground. His nose was bleeding and he was hurting all over. The deer had torn the door completely from the crib and almost killed Doe in the process.

We looked all winter for a huge buck with splinters hanging from his horns, but never located him, and he never came back to the crib, as far as we knew.

26

The Day Someone Almost Got Shot

FINCHBURG was noted for its abundance of wild game, especially quail. It was not hard to find twenty coveys of birds in one day and not have to cover much ground. A friend of the family, by the name of Walter Bowden, owned a hardware store in Monroeville. He was an avid hunter, especially of quail hunting. He loved to hunt on the Williams plantation in Finchburg.

One chilly, sunshiny day, Walter and a friend of his arrived around mid-morning for a day of quail hunting. Granddaddy was sitting by the potbellied stove in the store, when Walter and his friend walked in. Granddaddy told Walter how glad he was to see him, because he had wanted a good mess of quail. Walter's friend's face lit up, knowing that he was welcomed to hunt, and if the quail were as plentiful as Walter had said, then getting a mess of birds would be no problem.

Granddaddy told Thomas to go and open the gate to the field below the store, and they could start hunting there. In those days, almost every bird hunter used a Browning Automatic that held five shells. It was nothing for two hunters to empty ten shots on a covey rise and most of the time pick up four to six birds. When the dogs were let out and Thomas closed the gate, the two dogs started winding birds and were soon on point.

The two hunters flushed the covey, and each picked up three birds. In those days, we never hunted for singles, because it was too easy to find a new covey. The hunters approached a long sloping hill, which led to a branch head. There was thick coverage along the branch, so the hunters could not see the other side. Halfway down the hillside the dogs pointed, and the birds flushed and headed toward the branch. The hunters fired five quick shots each.

You have never heard such hollering and screaming in your lifetime. The hunters could hear a loud screaming voice; just on the other side of the branch head, out of sight.

"Lord Jesus, I is shot, please save me."

"Oh, my." Walter looked at his friend and said, "You have just shot somebody."

The guest could not believe what he was witnessing, and asked

Bird dog on point.

Walter how he knew that his shots were the ones that hit someone. Walter looked at him and said, "Because I did not shoot."

The guest was so shaken up, he did not know if Walter had fired or not. The screaming ceased, and Walter said, "Let's cross the branch and see who you shot."

The guest said, "You reckon they are dead?"

Walter did not help anything by replying that they had quit yelling, so something bad must be wrong. They crossed the branch and quickly saw a fire, a wash pot, and clothes scattered all over the side of the branch. The wash pot was turned upside down; one woman's shoe was among the scattered clothes. No one could be found. After a thorough search all around the wash pot and fire, the hunters decided to go up the hill to a house, and inquire if anyone had seen anybody shot come up the way. Uncle Frank was sitting on the porch smoking his pipe. Walter said, "Uncle, did anybody come by here that had been shot?"

"No sir, but two women came by here running and scared to death. They went yonder way, but I do not think they were hurt."

What happened was, the two women were down at the spring washing clothes, and did not know there was a living soul anywhere around. When the ten shots went off, they did not know what had happened and did not stay around to see. The woman stirring the pot with the clothes in it ran straight over it, turning it upside down. The other woman that was folding the clothes turned the bucket of washed clothes over, in making her hasty retreat. Walter said to the guest, "I sure hope you haven't killed one of Captain Dick's tenants."

The guest was already upset, and this statement did not help his feelings at all. The guest never hit another bird all day.

The women finally returned home later that afternoon. Their wash pot was moved to an area on the branch that had an opening in the tree line, which would enable one to see both sides of the branch.

27

Old Red's Finchburg Fox Hunt

A LL the kids in the surrounding farms always looked forward to Saturday night. Saturday night was fox hunting night. The ladies would prepare a huge picnic lunch or carry food to be cooked in the woods. The men would pool their fox dogs, and meet at a farm, which was owned by Mrs. Whisenhunt, a widow who lived in a huge, old-fashioned dogtrot house. A dogtrot was an open hallway running through the center of the house, with a porch on both ends, and one set of steps ran from the ground up to the center of the porch in front of the dogtrot with another set of steps going down in the back. Houses in this area were built this way so as to accommodate the children, with the girls' rooms on one side and the boys' rooms on the other side. The dogtrot also served for good ventilation during the hot summer nights. A cool breeze was always present, blowing through the dogtrot.

Widow Whisenhunt lived by herself and was hard-of-hearing, but she was a loving person who always enjoyed visitors. Her land was ideal for fox hunting, and we knew we were always welcome. The men always built a huge fire down the lane from Mrs. Whisenhunt's house, and everyone gathered around, especially the women and children. Mrs. Whisenhunt had arthritis and could not get about very well, so she sat in an old straight chair on the porch in the center of the dogtrot where she would listen to the dogs.

Foxhunters always bragged about their dogs. On this particular night, a Mr. Pearson from Monroeville begged Uncle Fonde to let him bring his dog, Old Red. He wanted everyone to see how good he was, and how he was usually the first to bark on the fox track. The fire was built, the women were busy with cooking, and we children were having the time of our lives.

The men all met in a circle, holding their dogs on leashes. Uncle Fonde told Mr. Pearson, since he had such a good dog, he would have the honor of turning Old Red loose first. This thrilled Mr. Pearson to no end, and he kept repeating how good Old Red was and to just listen for him to strike.

Old Red was turned loose, and down the hill he went. In a few minutes, Old Red let out a series of barks, and Mr. Pearson said, "Just listen to Old Red. He's burning that fox up."

All the men started wondering why their dogs were not running the fox with Old Red. About twenty minutes into the hunt, several of the dogs struck a fox scent a great distance from where Old Red was barking. Mr. Pearson told the other guys, he could not understand why their dogs had not joined Old Red. All this time, Old Red was barking and howling but did not seem to be going anywhere.

The other dogs jumped the fox, and a race was on. Old Red was still barking, so Uncle Fonde told Murry, the dog man, to walk under the hill to see if he could figure out what Old Red was running. Murry walked down the hill to check on Old Red. Mr. Pearson bragged all the way down the hill before getting to the dog. The men shined the light toward Old Red and his barking.

Mr. Pearson could not believe what he saw. Old Red was hung in the top of the fence and was barking his head off. Mr. Pearson got Old Red out of the fence, and up the hill he went, with Old Red in his arms. The men could not help but holler to Mr. Pearson, saying what a good voice Old Red had. To my knowledge, Mr. Pearson never came back fox hunting again, and if by chance he met one of the hunters in town, he made it a point to cross over to the opposite side of the street, to keep from meeting him face on.

Meanwhile, the ladies had the food and hot coffee ready. Everyone got a plate, and the ladies piled the food on. Uncle Fonde got the ladies to fix Mrs. Whisenhunt a plate, and he walked up the road to deliver it. The old lady was sitting in her chair, trying to hear the hounds. By this time, the other dogs had packed and were really running the old fox.

Upon hearing Uncle Fonde's approach to the house, Mrs. Whisenhunt lit her kerosene lantern and sat it by her chair. She was so glad to see Uncle Fonde, especially since he had her a plate piled high with food. After a few minutes of conversation, Uncle Fonde started back to the fire, where the food was being served. But the dogs were getting closer and coming straight toward Mrs. Whisenhunt's house, barking every breath of the way. Uncle Fonde, about twenty steps away from her porch, saw the fox scoot under the steps right beneath where the old lady was sitting.

The dogtrot house where Mrs. Whisenhunt was sitting when the fox hounds knocked her backwards.

The dogs, running full speed, went up the steps instead of under them, with the entire pack hitting the old lady full force, knocking her halfway down the dogtrot. She always smoked a corncob pipe, and all Uncle Fonde could see was sparks from her pipe, and the pack of dogs running down the back steps. The old lady was getting up on her knees just as Uncle Fonde got to her. All she said was, "Fonde, that was a good race, but did you know that those damn dogs ran right over me, and I still can't locate my cob pipe?"

Dr. Charles Rutherford, holding Sharmon Rutherford, and Quill Abney with turkey. Quill was well known for his guiding and calling ability. They are standing in front of Dr. Charles's home in Franklin, Alabama.

28

Their Neighbor's Wife

ONE of our neighbors owned a large plantation several miles away, with a huge colonial style home in the center of it. In the backyard, just across the back fence, about sixty yards from the house, was a two-bedroom log cabin. This is where the cook lived with her husband and eight children. Bertha was the cook's name, and Shultz was her husband's name. Bertha was much younger than her husband, who had a history of heart trouble and was unable to do anything that required much physical effort.

On one side of the house, down a lane, lived Quill with his wife and eight children. He was an able-bodied man, who was blessed with the ability to call wild turkeys, when others had failed, by using a wing bone. Quill was in big demand by city turkey hunters who wanted to use him as their guide. When Shultz was away, Quill was always checking on Shultz's wife to make sure that she was okay.

On the other side of the house lived Boot and Liza. They had eleven children. Boot was also a very good turkey guide and he also tried to check on Shultz's wife, not knowing that Quill was checking on her.

One dark night, Shultz had gone to Mobile for several days, so Quill and Boot both independently decided to check on Bertha.

Quill moved toward the house from one direction, and Boot, on the opposite side of the house, moved toward the house another way. The night was dark, and no way would they use a flashlight, because they did not know when Shultz would return. They both had made the trip so many times in the black of night, that every foot of ground leading to Bertha's house was very well known by both men.

Each man slipped through the dark, neither knowing the other was anywhere around. Just as each approached the center of the backyard of Bertha's house, in the black of the night, they ran into each other, knocking each other to the ground. They got up running in opposite directions. One hit the rail fence on one side of the house, and the other tore three strings of barbed wire from the fence on the other side of the yard. Bruised and cut, they both had some hard explaining to do to their wives, as to what had happened to them. From that night on, they visited Bertha's house during daylight.

29

The Sunday Morning Fox Hunt

SATURDAY night was always fox hunting time for Uncle Fonde and Murry, regardless if anyone else went. One Saturday night, Uncle Fonde and Murry went by themselves and had several good races during the night. In fact, the dogs were still running at 10:30 a.m. on Sunday morning. Forehand Church, a black church, happened to be having their once-a-month service on this morning. The last thing Uncle Fonde and Murry wanted was for their pack of foxhounds to interrupt church in any way.

The dogs were burning the fox up. Several times they were seen across the road, behind the church, around the church, and through the churchyard. The congregation had entered the church, and the service had started. The church was old, and several boards had separated from the side wall. Uncle Fonde and Murry tried every way possible to catch the dogs before they came back to the church. But it was impossible to stop them as they headed straight for the church. The fox ran under the church and then into the wall of the church, where the boards were torn loose. Some of the dogs began tearing at the loose boards, trying to get to the fox. Several others went through the half-open front door.

The congregation did not know what was going on, and most of them ran out the door, not waiting to see. Needless to say, church services were broken up. Uncle Fonde sent Murry to the churchyard to try and retrieve the dogs, while he stayed out of sight down the road.

At the next church meeting, Murry was put on the prayer list, and a twenty-dollar bill was donated anonymously to the church.

30

Lightning Strikes Little Bud

L ITTLE Bud was one of my fishing partners. He was always ready to go, and we fished for all species. The only time he was ready to quit fishing before I was ready was if a storm with lightning appeared. He was afraid of bad weather and would leave the water if he could get to the riverbank.

What we referred to as a boat landing in those days consisted of a foot trail leading down the steep riverbank to the water's edge. In those days, no one would bother any boat left tied along the river's banks, and it was always available when we needed it. We did not have an outboard motor, but we did not need one because good fishing was within easy paddling distance of each landing.

My favorite fishing area was located close to what we referred to as the upper swamp. It was a rock island about one-half acre in size and about forty yards from the riverbank toward the middle of the river. From the riverbank to the island's bank was a large eddy of calm water, infested with underwater rocks, which made it a haven for bluegill and feeding crappies. Around the island was swift running water where spotted bass and catfish could be caught. This was our secret fishing hole for years, and very few people knew about it.

One summer morning, Granddaddy let Doe drive us to the swamp in the truck. Little Bud lived on the way to the swamp, so we

The island on the Alabama River. This was one of our favorite fishing areas on the river.

picked him up, along with a sack, two buckets of earthworms, and his two Calcutta fishing poles. (Calcutta was a local name given to all swamp-grown bamboo plants located along the streams and swamps of southwest Alabama.) I had a minnow seine that we used to catch live minnows. Our minnow bucket was a five-gallon lard can with nail holes punched in the top to give the minnows air.

This particular morning we went to a branch in the swamp that always held plenty of minnows. The banks and bottom of the branch were clean, and we had very little trouble seining enough minnows for a day's fishing. We soon had a lard can full of live minnows and headed for the landing. Doe carried the heavy lard can of minnows down the narrow lane that led to the boat and placed it in the center of the boat. Little Bud and I followed with the boat paddles and fishing tackle. Doe said that he would come back later that afternoon and pick us up. The rock island was downriver, so the paddling was easy going downstream, especially when there was a good current. We arrived at the island and baited a pole with one of our live

Little Bud
Johnson,
my fishing
and
hunting
companion.

minnows. The minnow did not hit the water good before the cork
moved and out of sight beneath the water it went. In what seemed
like five minutes, I landed a nice spotted bass. Within the next hour,
we had caught several bass and a nice mess of crappie. We floated
into the eddy side of the rock island and tied the front end of the boat
to one of a few willow bushes growing on the island. We baited our
lines with wigglers and earthworms and fished over the submerged
rocks in the eddy water. We caught bluegill and shell crackers all
morning. It was getting close to lunchtime, so we paddled the boat
around the outside of the island, which faced the middle of the river.
Little Bud was sitting on the front seat in the boat with his back to

me, and I was in the back of the boat. We opened our canned goods and ate our lunch.

Before we could finish eating our lunch, a huge black rain cloud began approaching from the south. It was full of thunder and lightning and looked very bad. We could see the heavy rain coming up the river, and I knew it was too late to paddle for the landing. Little Bud was rolling his line onto his pole, holding it straight up in the air, and begging me to please hurry and get us to the riverbank. I told him not to hold his pole in the air because of lightning.

The rain started coming down in sheets. Lightning was popping all around us. I saw Little Bud in the front of the boat, reach and get the top of the five-gallon lard bucket. He was holding the lid with both hands over his head, trying to keep the rain off. As he was leaning forward, facing the front of the boat, with the five-gallon tin lid over his head, lightning struck very close by, and Little Bud almost jumped out of the boat.

I had a stiff cane pole lying by my side in the boat. I reached down, picked it up, and with all my strength raised the pole over my head, and with a downward motion hit dead center the tin lid, which was on top of Little Bud's head. He jumped clear out of the boat onto the island, knowing lightning had just struck him. His ears were ringing, and he was shaking his head. Needles to say I was laughing like the devil. It took me ten minutes to convince him that it was not lightning that had struck him, but my stiff fishing pole that had hit the lard can lid on top of his head. He was very mad at me, and promised to tell Granddaddy what a trick I had pulled on him.

From that day forward, when we were fishing in a boat, Little Bud always sat facing me, especially on a cloudy day.

31

Laying Uncle Ben to Rest

O LD Uncle Ben died, and was to be buried at St. Peter Church, several miles from the plantation. It was mid-August and the heat was awful. Thomas borrowed the big truck to carry anyone that wanted to go from the plantation to the funeral.

Aunt Mattie Bell, who was crippled from rheumatism, used a walking stick to get around with. She lived several miles up the road and depended on neighbors or friends to carry her to different events, such as funerals, church, and weddings. This funeral would be attended by many, and Aunt Mattie was not going to miss it.

Uncle Ben was known to travel in a fifteen-mile radius and had offspring in each community. It was said that if just his children and girlfriends showed up, they would fill the church. The funeral was to be held at 1 p.m., the hottest part of the day. Thomas picked Aunt Mattie up, and she joined the other twenty or so people on the big truck body. The truck arrived at 11:30 a.m. at the church. This was to ensure that all could get in and be seated.

The church was already hot, and the gathering crowd did not help matters. Thomas escorted Aunt Mattie as close as he could to the front of the church. She could hardly make it, even with Thomas's help and the aid of her old reliable walking stick. The crowd kept increasing as well as the temperature. Hand-held fans, advertising the local funeral home, were distributed throughout the church. Most of these were grabbed and put to use very soon after the crowd started increasing. A huge oak tree stood directly in front of the church door. Most of the men were standing around beneath the little shade given off by the tree, before entering the increasingly hot church. All of the windows in the church were shut, because they were stuck. This was due to the fresh coat of paint to the entire outside and windows of the church. They could not be raised to help with the ventilation.

As time for the funeral arrived, the church was packed and could not hold another person. The front door was closed by Deacon Esaw, and the service began. Several hymns were sung, and the preacher took over the pulpit. He was wiping sweat from his forehead with a handkerchief with one hand, and holding a Bible in the other hand. Just as the preacher started to say a few words, the loudest explosion you could imagine shook the church and rattled the closed windows.

The preacher looked for a back door, but was unable to find one, so he hid under the pulpit. Esaw was leading the congregation out the front door, which he hit with such force, that it tore the hinges from the building. Still running and holding the door in front of him, he ran straight into the huge oak in front of the church. The impact knocked him backward and unconscious. Aunt Mattie threw her stick straight up in the air and started running up the aisle toward the open space, where the door used to be. Someone hollered, "Aunt Mattie, you left your walking stick."

Aunt Mattie passed several others running toward the front door. She was heard to say, "Damn the stick, I'm getting out of here."

After everyone cleared the church, except for the body and the preacher, still hiding under the pulpit, everyone was trying to determine what had caused the worst explosion they had ever heard.

Several spotted the door in front of the oak tree. As they lifted the door, they were surprised to find Esaw beneath, with a bleeding nose and knocked completely unconscious.

After several minutes of investigating the area, Thomas walked over to the butane tank that was located near the church. He discovered the pop-off valve on the tank had blown off and had created the loud noise. The preacher suggested the body be removed, and they would continue with only graveside services. This suited everyone except Esaw, which was still unconscious, even after two buckets of cold water was poured over him.

Aunt Mattie was already in the truck and yelled, "Somebody go in that church and bring me my stick." Esaw finally came to and Aunt Mattie started relying on her stick for walking again.

Uncle Ben was put to rest, and the congregation returned home, shaken but safe.

32

A Hundred Pounds of Cotton

ONE summer Granddaddy offered T. B. and me five dollars for every hundred pounds of cotton we picked. This seemed like good money, especially since the tenants were paid $1.50 to $2 per hundred pounds. We knew we were going to make a pile of money. We each got a cotton sack and headed for the field across the road from the store. We just knew we could pick a hundred pounds each before dark.

We started picking as hard as we could go. T. B. with his one good arm, and the nub on the other hand, seemed to be picking more than I was. I started pulling bolls and all from the tall cotton stalks, leaving more cotton than I was picking. Around 10 a.m., the sun started bearing down. We were dying of thirst, so we left our sacks in the field and slipped around behind the barn to get water and cool off, hoping Granddaddy would not see us.

We stayed in the cotton field until Sarah Lee rang the huge dinner bell next to the back porch. The ringing of the bell meant for all field hands to come to the big house for dinner. Those out of hearing of the bell carried their dinner with them, usually in a syrup bucket. Lunch for them consisted of molasses and several huge biscuits or some cornbread. Sometimes a piece of cured meat was added, depending on the supply. The dining room for tenants was located toward the back of the house, with the kitchen separating it from the large dining room where Granddaddy and his guest always ate.

After eating, all the pickers would return to the fields until dark. Then they would go to the store to be weighed out and paid, according to the pounds of the cotton they had picked. Some could pick three hundred pounds a day, but this was an exception. The average cotton picked per person was about one hundred fifty pounds.

T. B. and I did not come near the average; in fact, we left our sacks in the field overnight, hoping that the dew would make our sacks weigh more. This went on for two weeks. Finally, Granddaddy insisted we bring our sacks in for weighing that night. The day had been long and hot. Late that afternoon, after inserting several large rocks with our mixed sack of cotton, we headed for the scales. After weighting, T. B.'s total was thirty-six pounds, and mine was twenty-

Weighing of individual cotton picked in a day.

eight. The total man-hours of picking were two weeks and two days. If we had picked all summer, it was doubtful if we would have had a hundred pounds between the two of us. Granddaddy knew this, and that is why he offered us such a price for picking a hundred pounds.

Grandaddy Williams on his favorite horse.

33

Looking for Crickets

NEXT to the store was an old garden plot that had not been used in several years. The weeds were growing thick and high, well over our heads. Granddaddy told Doe, T. B., and me that if we would get some hoes and chop down the weeds, then we could catch enough crickets to go fishing with.

"When you finish, I'll take you to the creek, and you all can catch a mess of fish for supper," he promised.

That was music to our ears, because we were always ready to go fishing. We chopped weeds as hard as we could, looking for crickets at the same time. We finally chopped the entire garden plot, without catching the first cricket.

In fact, we did not even see a cricket. Granddaddy called us to the store and gave us a cold soda water. He told us to get through with the drinks and we could go to the creek. He looked around and asked, "Where are the crickets?"

Sadly we had to admit, we had not caught any. Laughing to himself, he said that was okay. "You know, sometimes those crickets move to other patches, so you all try that patch of weeds by the barn."

We hurried as fast as we could chop, so we could catch enough crickets to fish with before dark set in. After finishing that patch, with a total of three crickets in the jar, it finally dawned on us that we had been taken.

Granddaddy told us that those crickets must have moved again. "And besides, it's getting too late to go to the creek. We'll try again some other day."

34

The Quail Hunting Lease

WE were all sitting on the porch of the store one October day, when a large new car came down the lane, toward the store. The car pulled up and parked. Three white men and Boot, the turkey guide, got out.

Boot said, "Captain Dick, these men is looking for quail hunting land to lease. Dr. Charles done already leased his land to them and he sent me down here with them to talk with you."

The men introduced themselves to Granddaddy and told him they were businessmen from Anniston, and were looking for some other hunting ground to lease. Granddaddy let them talk for awhile, then told them he did not think there was enough quail around to hunt. He told them if they would come down next weekend, they would be welcome to hunt and decide for themselves.

As Boot and the men left, Granddaddy told Thomas to go out to the barn to see if the old chicken coop was in good shape. Monday morning Granddaddy sent Thomas to get Boot. When Thomas arrived at Boot's house, the dogs were gone, so Thomas knew that Boot was not there, but he called to Lizza and asked where Boot was. Lizza and most of the eleven children came to the door and told Thomas that Boot had gone squirrel hunting, but would soon be back. It was not long before Boot, holding two squirrels and a possum, came up the lane leading to the house, with at least six dogs following him. Thomas told Boot that Granddaddy wanted to see him. Boot gave Lizza the possum and squirrels and got in the truck with Thomas.

When Boot arrived at the store, Granddaddy told Boot that next Saturday morning he wanted him at the store really early, before the hunters from Anniston arrived. He was to take some quail and turn them loose all around the fields behind the store.

Granddaddy knew a man that had pen-raised quail for sale in the lower end of the county. Boot and Thomas were to go and pick up two hundred live birds on Friday.

Friday morning arrived, and Thomas filled the truck with gas, loaded the chicken coop onto the pickup and went to pick up Boot. Later that afternoon Thomas and Boot arrived with the live quail and were told to put them in the barn for the night. The next morning, Boot was to take six pen-raised quail to each briar patch and turn them loose before daylight.

Just as Boot released the last of the birds and started toward the store, a huge thunderstorm brought at least two inches of rain within an hour. It was still dark, as the rain began to let up some. Soon the hunters arrived, in two vehicles, with dog boxes that held four bird dogs per box, ready for a day of hunting.

Granddaddy apologized for the bad weather and tried to prepare them for the worst. They went on to say that some of their best hunts were in the rain or right after heavy rains. The dawn had started breaking, and the rain had almost stopped. The hunters loaded up, with Boot riding in the back of the first truck. They arrived at the edge of the first cornfield and turned two dogs out. The cornrows were full of water, and Boot explained that the quail were still near their roosts in the briar patches.

The dogs went to the first briar patch and came to a perfect point. The hunters approached with guns ready, but no birds flushed. As the dogs walked ahead, one bird got up about two feet

Dr. Charles Rutherford and Quill Abney. Dr. Rutherford sent Boot Davis with the quail hunters to talk with grandaddy about leasing hunting rights at Finchburg.

from the ground and went right back down before any of hunters could get a shot. Another bird got up, and one of the hunters fired, killing the quail. Both dogs were sent to retrieve the dead bird. Both dogs returned with a bird each, one alive and the other one dead. The hunters looked at Boot and asked if two birds had fallen.

Boot thought quickly and said, "That rain done wet some of them birds so bad they can hardly fly, and that dog caught one."

This went on most of the morning. However, the sun came out, drying things off, and the dogs did not catch the live birds so easily. The hunters could not believe the abundance of quail in each briar patch. The hunters ate lunch in the field, anxious to continue the hunt. Boot suggested they move to another field for the afternoon hunt.

The new field had some standing corn stalks with broom sage in the surrounding corners of the field. Two dogs were turned out and soon were winding birds. Both dogs locked up on a solid point. All excited, the hunters walked behind the dogs, hoping to get a good covey rise. The covey got up so fast that the hunters did not have time to get a shot off. Being used to the slow, wet birds that morning, they could not understand why they were flying so fast that after-noon. The same thing happened on the next covey rise. No shots were fired, and they all turned to Boot for an explanation.

"What's done happened is them birds done dried out from all that rain and now fly like they suppose too," he explained.

Soon the hunters adjusted to the change in the birds' actions,

Boot Davis, the morning of the rainstorm and hunt.

not realizing that the morning hunt was made up of pen-raised birds. However, that afternoon they had started to get a few shots at the wild coveys.

At the end of the hunt, Boot carried the hunters back by the store. Granddaddy asked if they had any luck. Boot threw two bags of quail on the store porch. Both bags were full of quail, most still wet from the morning downpour. Granddaddy told Thomas to take the quail down to Ned's house and he would dress them.

He explained, "When you come back to hunt in the morning, your quail will be ready, and we will discuss working out a lease. You will have to leave before lunch, because some bankers and doctors from Mobile are coming in to hunt and discuss leasing."

All three hunters tried to talk at once. They wanted to lease today and not take a chance of being overbid. They offered Granddaddy four times more money than he thought the lease was worth. Granddaddy hesitated, and the hunters quickly upped the price on the lease. Winking at Boot, Granddaddy said he hated to lease for such a low price, but would take it if they would sign a four-year lease. The hunters wrote a check, gave Boot a big tip, and all were happy.

Boot later told Granddaddy that all the hunters could talk about was what a deal they had made, and they had never seen such an abundance of quail on any place before coming here.

35

My Worst Belly Ache

BUDDY Boy was Uncle Fonde's only child and my first cousin. I was one year to the day older than Buddy Boy was. We played, hunted, and fished all over the plantation. We had many black playmates, so we were never in need of companionship or ideas as to what we would get into next. Buddy Boy did not like work any more than I did, so we tried to stay out of sight, entertaining ourselves all over the woods or along the creek banks. We planned one last, large fishing expedition before school started.

Whenever I spent the night with Uncle Fonde and Aunt Bonnie, I always slept in the same bed with Buddy Boy, upstairs in their old colonial style home. We would usually wrestle and talk half the night, until Uncle Fonde would come up the long stairs and make us go to sleep.

Buddy Boy had slipped a huge bag of English walnuts into the bedroom. We divided them with each other. I immediately started eating my share as soon as I cracked them and extracted the meat. Buddy Boy was steadily cracking walnuts and picking out the meat, but he did not seem to be eating any. I soon finished my share and noticed that Buddy Boy was neatly placing his walnut meat in a pile under his pillow. Every time he looked away, I would reach under the pillow and grab a handful of his walnuts. This went on for several minutes, and Buddy finally shelled his last walnut. He reached under the pillow to get some. He fumbled with the pillow, throwing cover everywhere and screamed as loud as he could, realizing that I had stolen his walnuts and eaten them. The fight broke out, awaking Uncle Fonde and Aunt Bonnie. Uncle Fonde separated us and threatened a good whipping, if we did not go to sleep and start behaving ourselves.

Buddy Boy was still fuming, but soon sleep overtook us as we both fell into a deep sleep. Early the next morning Uncle Fonde came upstairs and got us out of bed. After a huge breakfast, we loaded into the back of Uncle Fonde's truck, along with our fishing poles and tackle. He drove us to the creek, stopping long enough to pick up our companions, Papa and Bee, both about our age. We were told we would have to walk home, because everyone would be working and too busy to take time out to pick us up.

We seined the nearby branch and caught a lard bucket full of live minnows. We all spread out near the mouth of the creek where it ran into the Alabama River and started fishing. The fish were really hitting, especially skipjacks, which are too bony to eat, but lots of fun to catch. Suddenly I became nauseated; a hot flushing feeling overcame my entire body, and my stomach began to hurt the likes of which I had never experienced before. I started hollering, rolling over and over on the leaves along the creek bank, calling Buddy Boy for dear life. They all came running, just about as scared as I was. We were two miles from the nearest house and five miles from the store. Buddy Boy, Bee, and Papa took turns trying to help me walk out.

I would walk several steps and fall. They would help me up, and I would double over with pain in my right side and fall back to the ground. Buddy Boy left Bee and Papa with me and started running for Eddie's house, which was a good two miles away. After telling Eddie what was wrong, they caught the mule and came after me. They put me on the mule and started leading us out toward the store. Every step the mule made caused my side to hurt twice as much.

After several hundred yards, I fell off the mule and rolled into the ditch. Buddy Boy jumped on the mule and left for the store as fast as the old mule would go, seeking help for me.

Bee and Papa had broken sweet gum limbs and were fanning me. I would pass out from pain, come to and roll over and over, trying to get some relief. I could hear Papa ask Bee if I was dying.

Bee said, "I don't know, but he shore looks like it."

This seemed to make the pain worse, and I began to feel like I was dying. After what seemed like hours, Uncle Fonde arrived, and they loaded me into the pickup and carried me to the new hospital in Monroeville. Dr. Stallworth operated and found what he had suspected: a very hot appendix that was ready to rupture.

After this experience, we were never allowed to go hunting or fishing without some means of transportation; most of the time, it was a mule and wagon.

36

Our Hunting and Fishing Truck

GRANDDADDY bought us an old stripped down Model A Ford truck, with no cab and a small body. It was just large enough to hold us and our tackle or guns, depending on what we were going to do. Peewee was the only one that could drive the truck, so Granddaddy felt safe with Peewee going with us. The old truck never had much in the way of brakes and most of the time none at all. When the brakes failed, we all jumped off or held on for dear life until the truck would come to a halt.

One day we were all on the truck, cruising down the river bank road, anticipating a full day of fishing. As we went around a mud puddle, trying not to get stuck, Peewee jerked the steering wheel to the left to get back in the road. The whole steering wheel came off in Peewee's hands. We all jumped from the truck, just as it left the road and headed straight for the river. The only thing keeping the truck and Peewee from going into the river was a large sycamore tree, which the truck centered.

It was a long walk back to the store, and the end of our fishing trip for that day.

37

How Not to Cook a Turkey

NIG shot a turkey hen one morning and tried to cook her before Granddaddy caught him. Nig was allowed to kill a gobbler when he wanted one to eat, but nobody was to kill a wild turkey hen. Nig had an old pressure cooker, probably one of the first ones made. It worked great, unless the pop-off valve was not functioning. He picked the feathers off the turkey, leaving her feet on, and put her in the pressure cooker. The old wood stove's eye was red hot, but he added more wood, so he could quickly get the job over with. He closed the lid as tight as it would go. Some steam was beginning to escape from the safety valve, as Nig took two good slugs of his moonshine and went to the front porch to sit in the sun and wait for his turkey to cook.

The sun and the moonshine soon took effect, and Nig went into a deep sleep. Manzie rode up in the wagon, on the way to the swamp to get a load of wood. He got off the wagon and started up the front steps to awaken Nig. Just as he reached the top step, the whole house sounded as if it had blown up. Smoke and steam covered the entire house. Nig jumped clear off the porch and ran into the barbed wire fence across the road. Manzie fell from the top step backward, got up, and ran toward the mule and wagon, only to see the back-end of each as they went over the hill.

After the smoke and steam cleared, Manzie and Nig built up enough courage to go into the house to see what had happened. As they entered the house and started toward the kitchen, they both looked at each other, and at the same time said, "Ain't no kitchen here!"

The pressure cooker had malfunctioned, because the fire was way too hot, and the safety valve had stuck, causing the whole thing to blow up, leaving only a part of the roof on the kitchen. Manzie looked at Nig and said, "Br'er Nig, ain't that a turkey foot hanging from the board toward the hole in the roof. Shore do wonder where the rest of her is."

Manzie took a hard look at Nig and said, "I guess the rest of that turkey left with the kitchen roof."

The old pressure cooker that eliminated Nig's kitchen roof.

38

The Night the Sky Lit Up

UNCLE West was in his eighties, too old to hunt and fish, but always ready with a story, or many stories, depending on how long someone would listen. Uncle West lived on a hill overlooking the swamp, with the road to the river and creek passing by his front door. I always made a point of going into the swamp on the road that passed through Uncle West's front yard. This gave me an opportunity to stop and listen to the stories of the old days on the plantation.

One of his best stories took place around 1916. The headlines of the *Mobile Press* for several days had told of a huge blimp (dirigible) flying up the river from Mobile on its way to Montgomery. The headlines were published as an advertisement of the event, and also to warn the people living along its route what to expect. What the paper did not realize was the fact that most if not all of us had never seen anything flying except birds. Furthermore, if a newspaper was ever seen in Finchburg, it was many months after the original circulation date. The only reason Granddaddy knew about this great event was the battery-operated radio mentioned it on the news release. It stated that a blimp was coming up the river, but gave no date.

Uncle West said that on a Tuesday night in March, the entire plantation could hear a rumbling in the sky, and it seemed to be moving their way. The sky was dark, but the stars were shining. They did not notice a bolt of lightning or any dark cloud in the sky, yet the rumbling was getting closer. Everyone on the plantation ran outside to see which way the storm was moving. All of a sudden, a huge dark-looking object appeared over the trees. Bright lights were shining underneath the object. The people that stayed around long enough could see people walking around underneath the object, with their arms waving to the people below.

The engines were making a roaring noise that had not been heard before by the people in Finchburg. Pig, our main cook, hollered, "The time has come. Go ring the bell at the church."

Uncle Buck said, "Damn the bell," as he headed for the woods, stripping barbed wire off the fences as he ran. Women and children ran and hid under the haystacks; the mules and cows broke all the fences down, and some were never seen again. Dogs that did not run began to growl, and chickens left the roost. The huge thing, making so much racket with such bright lights, soon passed over the plantation, continuing north up the river.

The next day some were brave enough to come out from under the haystacks, especially the women and children. Some of the men took several days to get back home, with most of their clothes torn by saw-briars and barbed wire.

The Good Hope Church was overcrowded on Sunday, with standing room only. The crowd was larger than any big meeting, and many were saved that day, or tried to be.

39

The Morning the Lord Showed Up

BOOT, the turkey-hunting guide with the eleven children, very seldom had the opportunity to hunt alone. There were always hunters to guide, and most of the time he never carried a gun. Boot's boss, Lizza (who was also the mother of his eleven children), did not allow any hunting on Sunday. Boot and Lizza lived in the hill section of Davis Landing on Dr. Rutherford's plantation. Behind Boots's house, looking west toward the Alabama River, was a huge ridge overlooking the river, which most of the local residents called Nancy Mountain. This was the tallest hill known in the area. If you did not believe it to be so, then you might have become one of the many hunters who were fooled into walking from one side to the other. Many never doubted its reputation, after trying to conquer the walk, and they never returned for a second hike.

Every morning in the spring of the year, an old gobbler would sound off before day, and he was always located in the same direction, morning after morning. His gobble was unusual, starting with a coarse gobble and tapering off with a shrill gobble. This sound could easily be heard from Boot's front porch, and there was no doubt that it was the same old turkey, because of this familiar series of gobbles. This old turkey would irritate the devil out of Boot. Boot always thought that no wild turkey could resist his call on a wing bone, and he was determined to bag the Nancy Mountain boss of all turkeys.

Remember that this took place in the early 1940s, when in such rural areas even an airplane passing overhead caused much excitement for the entire population. On this particular Sunday morning, Boot was the first one out of the house at 3:30 a.m., and was in a quick rush to the outhouse, due to the call of nature. On the way to the outhouse, he heard a loud series of gobbles coming from the middle of Nancy Mountain. Boot wanted to listen, but there were more important matters at hand. Finishing his call of nature, he started back to the house. The old turkey was still gobbling, especially when an owl would hoot, and he would then give a double or triple gobble.

Boot could not stand it anymore; he knew Lizza would give him the devil, but he had to see for himself if the old bird was as sharp as his gobble. Boot eased into the house, trying to dodge the children, who were sleeping everywhere on pallets in the three-room house. If he were careful, he could retrieve his clothes and his gun, and then exit without making any noise. He also envisioned taking that old gobbler and being back home before Lizza and the children arose from a good Saturday night's sleep.

Boot made his exit without awakening any of the family. It was about 4 a.m., and the old gobbler was still gobbling every few minutes. To walk to the old turkey would take forty-five minutes, so he did not hesitate. Boot arrived at the foot of Nancy Mountain, just in time, right before daybreak, and in time for the old turkey to fly down. While it was still dark, but light enough to see, Boot positioned himself in an old treetop at the foot of the mountain. The old gobbler would answer any noise, from the bullfrogs in an old swamp pond, to the squeak of the great blue heron, as he glided up the river looking for a pond where he could feed on minnows and tadpoles.

Boot waited until the first crow sounded, which was a sign to the old turkey hunter that it was time to call to the old gobbler. He knew

Boot Davis with wife Liza and his eleven children in front of their home near Nancy Mountain.

he could do this without scaring him. Boot gave three small yelps on his wing bone yelper. The old gobbler answered with a triple gobble. According to the rules of turkey hunting, this was the perfect situation for returning the yelper to his pocket, and waiting for the old bird to fly down within range for a clear shot. The crows cawed, the woodpeckers started making their usual sounds, and the wood ducks squealed. Anything that made a familiar noise caused the old gobble to sound off again.

Daylight arrived, and a distant rumble of an oncoming thunderstorm could be heard. The old gobbler would answer every sound of thunder, but did not move from his limb where he was roosting. It was well past flying-down time, and Boot knew from past experience the old gobbler would fly down any moment. Boot also knew that Lizza would be up at any moment back at the house, but he had gone through too much to give up now, regardless of what Lizza would say or do when he returned home.

The thunder increased and was soon coming over the top of the mountain. Shortly, a black cloud appeared over the top of the mountain, causing the sky to darken like Boot had never seen before. The old gobbler would answer with a gobble with each bolt of lightning and rumble of thunder. The black cloud covered the entire top of the mountain. Boot was scared and could only think of Lizza telling him that the Lord did not believe in Sunday hunting. Over the loud claps of thunder, a strange noise could be heard. It first sounded like a huge roar, with a popping noise that had never been heard before by Boot. The old turkey went silent, and all Boot could hear was the roar and popping sound coming over the top of the mountain.

Boot, still hiding in the fallen treetop, glanced up toward the sky. As he looked toward the roaring noise and the popping sound, he wanted to run, but did not know which way. All of a sudden, this black object, with what he thought were hands waving, and a man or something under the object, appeared over the trees, on top of the mountain, and headed straight for him. The black cloud was roaring along with whatever that was coming after him. The rain and wind came also about this time.

Boot stood it as long as he could. He left his gun in the treetop, ran the three miles up the opposite end of Nancy Mountain, and fell across the front porch. Lizza hearing all the commotion on the front porch went to the door. There was Boot with his overalls in threads, and briars hanging from his coat.

She hollered, "What in the world ails you?"

Boot, still out of breath, managed to tell Lizza that she would never have to worry about him hunting on Sunday again, "Cause the Lord done come over that mountain, in that black sky, waving his hands, and headed straight for me."

Lizza said, "Fool, I done told you 'bout hunting on Sunday."

About that time, a black helicopter flew low toward the house. Boot and Lizza, both hollered, saying, "Here he comes again." Both tried to get through the door at the same time. Lizza pushed Boot back onto the porch, telling him that he was the cause of the Lord's coming, so go out there and talk to Him. Boot finally got in through the side window and joined Lizza and the children under the bed. The helicopter went over the house and was soon out of sight. Two hours later Lizza told Boot to peep outside the door and see if it was gone.

It was several months before Boot found out what that black object was, but he never hunted on Sunday again. He was one of the first people in Finchburg to see a helicopter.

40

Running Something We Never Saw

SATURDAYS were always a day of hunting with slingshots, a pocketful of rocks for ammunition, and six to ten dogs following us into the woods. The hunters included Buddy Boy, Frazer, T. B., Doe, Leslie, and me. It's a good thing that rocks were cheap, because we all shot several pocketfuls during one of these hunts. We would always leave the store just after breakfast and work our way through the fields toward the woods, seeking our main game—rice birds, jay birds, thrash, woodpeckers, robins, and field larks. Occasionally a rabbit that was too slow to outrun the dogs or one that would go into a hole, allowing us to twist him out, was also on the list. Once in a while, we would jump a stray house cat.

Granddaddy had a half-collie, half-shepherd dog that was always ready to follow us. The dog's name was Tip, and he hated stray house cats, and did not let many of them get away from him. I can look back now and see why most house cats stayed close to home.

In those days, World War II was really heating up. Everything was rationed, and some things were impossible to get, especially old pure rubber inner tubes. The best were red in color and made an ideal slingshot. Whoever was the lucky person to find a discarded red inner tube along the road was the best-liked kid on the plantation.

We made two types of slingshots. One was a single-stock, made with a stick and one straight piece of inner tube, which had an old shoe tongue attached to the rubber for holding the rock. This type was dangerous, because it was easy to hit your thumb if you did not hold it just right. The other type was called a double stock, which was made out of a forked stick or was whittled from a board. This make was the most desired, because you rarely hit your thumb, and it produced twice as much power, because of the two pieces of rubber.

I remember Frazer, who was almost as fat as I was, planned the hunt. The hunt was to take place a long way down on a creek, deep in the thick woods. Frazer assured us that it was full of game. The dogs were in the lead, and we boys were just behind them, not wasting time in getting to the creek bottom. Old Tip gave a series of barks and the other dogs got into the race.

We had just started running toward the dogs, when all of a sudden, the loudest scream that we had ever heard came from the direction of the creek, where the dogs were running. We all came to a sudden stop, with T. B. asking what that was. Just about that time,

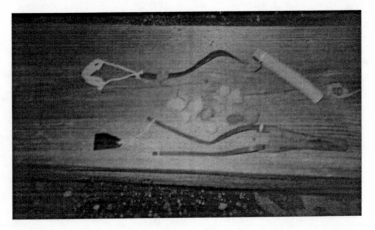

Our hurting weapons consisted of sling shots. Pictured are both models: a single stock and a double stock. The ammunition was a pocketful of rocks picked up along the way.

the loud scream came nearer. The entire pack of dogs met us, coming up the hill with their tails tucked between their legs. None of the dogs slowed down as they went by us. Another scream sounded like it was just about where we were at the moment. Frazer was the first to run, with the rest of us not too far behind. We scattered in all directions, running for our lives. Whatever made the noise was never seen, and we never went back to find out about it.

We were all out of breath as we approached the store. Frazer and I were running last because of our being overweight. The dogs had run under the store porch. Granddaddy wanted to know what we were running from.

We were not about to tell him that something had run us out of the woods. Thinking quickly, I told him we were racing to see who could get to the store first. Granddaddy remarked, with one of his light grins, that the dogs had won the race by ten minutes.

41

Walter Outshoots the Salesman

MR. Walter Bowden asked Granddaddy if he could come over on Thursday, bring a friend and do some quail hunting. Walter ran a hardware store, and one of the salesmen that called on him was said to be one of the best quail shots in the state, and maybe in the South. Walter could not stand anyone beating him shooting or fishing. Granddaddy gave Walter permission, so he called the salesman and told him that they would hunt on the upcoming Thursday.

Thursday was a beautiful, cool fall day; the sun was bright, and very little wind was blowing. The hunters came by the store to speak and to let Granddaddy know they would be hunting.

The hunt started behind the store, where we always found birds. I can remember hunting all day while never getting out of sight of the store, and having constant quail for shooting. We could hear shooting all morning, so we knew they were finding birds. At lunchtime the hunters returned to the store to eat some canned goods. We could tell that Walter was mad, but we did not know the reason. He finally admitted that the salesman had eight birds to his two.

The afternoon hunt was not much better from Walter's perspective, and as the sun was setting the hunters returned to the car and counted the birds that each had killed. Walter had five, and the salesman had the limit of fifteen. Walter did not say much, but you could tell he was not very happy. He asked Granddaddy if he could bring the salesman on another hunt. The salesman was thrilled to death to be invited on another hunt. Walter told the salesman to be at his house early Thursday morning, and they would hunt all day.

The day of the second hunt arrived, and Walter was determined to outshoot the salesman on this day and get even for the last hunt.

The hunters arrived and parked next to a fence adjoining a cornfield. The dogs were turned out and immediately winded birds. With tails wagging and very careful slipping, the dogs went under the barbed fence, and locked on a perfect point, just ten yards on the

Walter Bowden holding the turkey he killed in Finchburg, Alabama. He is also holding his favorite gun he referred to as "Ol' Bessy."

other side of the fence. Walter told the salesman to cross the fence first, in case the birds got up before both could cross the fence. Walter let the salesman get one foot and leg through the fence. At that moment his coat got hung, with one foot on one side and the other on the other side of the fence. Walter eased two shells in his old L. C. Smith double barrel, pointed it in the air and fired both barrels at once.

The salesman jumped through the fence, tearing his hunting coat and a large area from the seat of his pants. The salesman landed several feet on the ground on the other side of the fence. All he could say was "What the hell was that?"

Walter told him not to pay any attention to the noise. It was just old Bessie going off. He said he had no control over the gun since the safety was malfunctioning, sometimes firing both barrels without him even touching the trigger.

After the salesman dusted the dirt from his clothes and gathered some composure from the fright, Walter went through the fence, and the hunt proceeded. On the next covey rise, Walter downed three and the salesman none. He only got off one shot in all that time, as he kept cutting his eyes toward Walter and Old Bessie.

The salesman was so unnerved, that at the end of the day, Walter had fourteen birds and the salesman three.

42

Burying Part of My Best Friend

OUR water supply for the plantation was in a huge wooden tank, which was located halfway up a metal tower that had a windmill attached to its top. The windmill would pump the water from the well up into the wooden water tank for storage. If the wind was not adequate enough to turn the windmill, then the old Farm-All tractor equipped with a pulley and a long belt was put into use.

Thomas would crank the tractor and hook the belt to the pulley on the tractor. The opposite end of the belt was hooked to a pulley, which was connected to the water pump. The tractor was put into gear, and the pump would pump the water from the well into the tank, until the tank started overflowing with fresh well water. We were all warned not to ever go near the tractor and pulley while it was in operation. The exposed pulleys and belt were very dangerous.

One day, for some unknown reason, T. B. got a piece of haywire and eased it over the running tractor without being seen. Several minutes later we heard T. B. screaming for dear life. We all ran toward the sound and found T. B. with his arm crushed in the pulley with nothing but his thumb remaining attached to his hand. He was bleeding heavily, so Granddaddy quickly sent Thomas with T. B. to the hospital in Repton.

Dr. Carter and his wife. Dr. Carter ran the only hospital in the area. The hospital was located in Repton, Alabama.

Doe and I found the piece of haywire and three of T. B.'s fingers attached to the wire by a piece of skin. T. B. had stuck the wire into the pulley, and it had pulled his entire arm into the belt. We recovered the severed fingers and placed them in an empty Eat-Well sardine can and put them in the icehouse under a sack.

After several days in the hospital, T. B. was sent home to heal. Saturday was always a busy day around the store, and many of the workers on the plantation would spend all day Saturday trading in the store and sitting on the store porch, drinking soda water, eating sardines and crackers, and socializing throughout the day. Doe and I decided that when T. B. arrived at the store on Saturday morning, we would retrieve his fingers from the icehouse and have a funeral to bury his fingers.

T. B. arrived at the store with his arm and what was left of his hand still in bandages and heavily wrapped with gauze. Doe retrieved the fingers. Thomas dug the grave, and we buried T. B.'s fingers in the Eat-Well sardine can in front of the store, with almost all of the plantation workers looking on from the store porch.

We all told T. B. his fingers had gone to hell, and he had better try to behave and save the rest of his body for heaven.

43

The Annual Dove Hunt

G RANDDADDY always had one huge dove hunt every year. There was an old wet-weather pond located behind the store in the middle of several surrounding cornfields. Thomas was sent on a mission to burn all the vegetation around the pond, because doves love to eat burned-over grass seed. In a week's time, it seemed that every dove in the surrounding area, was feeding in the burned area. Bankers, doctors, merchants, politicians and kinfolks were invited. All were looking forward to Captain Dick's dove shoot.

The Mobile guests were made up of the elite bankers, professionals, and their guests. This crowd would always arrive in a caravan, well before daylight on the morning of the hunt. Granddaddy greeted the Mobile guests and called Mr. Barry Lyons, who was the president of First National Bank of Mobile and a good friend of Granddaddy's, over to the side and away from the crowd. Granddaddy told Barry that times were hard, and as much as he hated to admit it, he just did not have enough food to invite them for breakfast, but that he would try to scrape up enough canned goods for lunch. Mr. Lyons, who was the group's spokesman, told Dick not to worry about food, that they would enjoy the hunt and make out with canned goods for lunch.

Thomas escorted all of the hunters into the burned-over area well before daylight. It was very cold that morning, and the ground was frozen solid, along with the water in the old pond. After Thomas had gone to place the hunters in the fields, Granddaddy's teenage nephew drove up to the store from Monroeville. He ran into the store where Granddaddy was sitting by the warm potbellied stove and began to relate to Granddaddy how much he wanted to shoot doves, but that he did not have any shells. Granddaddy, halfway laughing to himself, asked what gauge gun he was shooting. Lyston Allen looked a little funny and replied, "Whatever gauge gun you will loan me. I left mine in Monroeville."

Granddaddy went into the office and returned with a 12-gauge rabbit-eared double barrel L. C. Smith with both barrels full choke. This was not the best choice for a dove gun, because it had plenty of power, but Lyston Allen did not know about such things.

Granddaddy gave Lyston Allen the gun and walked over to the stack of shells in the store corner. He looked for the right gauge shells, and chose the highest power shells being made at that time. All were high brass, loaded with number four shots, and enough powder to kill turkeys at fifty yards. Granddaddy gave his nephew four boxes of shells with instructions not to try to shoot those doves too far away, but wait until "they are almost on top of you before shooting," because these new low-powered shells would not reach out very far.

Lyson Allen was not a veteran hunter and did not know any better. He thanked Uncle Dick for the use of the gun and the four boxes of shells, and with anticipation of a great hunt walked over the frozen ground toward the dove shoot. Granddaddy yelled to him to kill a sack of doves and bring back the shells not used.

Somewhere around 10:30 a.m., Lyston Allen stumbled into the store, holding the borrowed gun in one hand and two boxes of unused shells in the other. He was the worst sight that you could imagine. His eyes were black, his nose was bleeding, and his right shoulder was in severe pain. He was almost crying.

Granddaddy looked at Lyston Allen, asking, "Boy, how many doves did you kill?"

The reply was, "Two and one-half doves, and I still have two boxes of shells left. The one-half bird lit in a tree thirty yards from me, and those low-powered shells still tore him in half."

Granddaddy looked at Lyston Allen and told Thomas to wash the blood from his bleeding nose. He told Lyston Allen to hurry back into the field with the remaining shells and at least kill enough for a meal.

Lyston Allen said, "Uncle Dick, Mama told me to be home before dinner, so I better get going. I shore did enjoy the hunt, but next time, I will bring my own shells and gun."

Lyston Allen Hixon, my granddaddy's nephew.

Old double barrel gun with high-powered shells.

It was dinnertime, and the hunters had all of the shooting they could stand. They were ready to sit and relax at the store with a meal consisting of sardines, Vienna sausages, pork and beans, and cheese and crackers. Granddaddy apologized for not having "a good hot meal cooked for them." He explained that he just did not have enough food to provide them with a decent meal. They all felt sorry for Captain Dick and told him how much they enjoyed canned goods for a change, trying to make him feel better.

Granddaddy called for Thomas to get the old jug from the back of the store, bring some glasses, and set them on the store counter within easy reach of the hunters. The weather was changing very rapidly, the temperature was dropping, and clouds were moving in. It was bringing both sleet and a small amount of snow to the plantation. Over the roar of the wood stove in the middle of the store, the sleet could be heard hitting the tin roof. The warmth of the old wood stove felt good as the hunters took turns downing glasses of the moonshine, which Thomas was pouring from the jug. Granddaddy told the crowd that his shinny was so mild, that no one ever needed a chaser. Most of the hunters, after taking a large drink, either faked the after-effect, or were not used to such strong drink. After several drinks, hunger pains were experienced, as they were talking loudly and laughing.

Granddaddy told the crowd, "Gentlemen, I can't let you eat canned goods without at least sitting down at a table. All of you take one more drink, and we'll go over to the house and eat at the big table. Be sure and get a good drink because Miss Lamb doesn't allow alcohol in the big house."

Most refused the offer, but a few decided on one more drink before eating. Thomas gathered the canned goods and delivered them to Sarah Lee in the kitchen where she opened the cans and placed the contents on the individual plates, which were spaced around the big table in the dinning room. Sarah Lee placed three large platters of hot cornbread on the table, with several molds of

The dove hunters from Mobile standing in the cold before Thomas escorted them into the field.

homemade butter near the bread.

Three gallons of cold buttermilk were placed within easy reach of everyone. A large plate of sliced raw onions was added to the table, along with several plates of soda crackers. Granddaddy asked the entire assembly to be seated and requested that Mr. Barry Lyons return thanks. Two of the hunters missed their chairs and sat on the floor, both blaming it on a bad case of vertigo. The blessing was said, and all of the hunters began to eat.

Some did not know if they were eating sardines or Viennas, since the moonshine had started to take effect on them. All of the guests drank huge glasses of cold buttermilk and ate hot buttered cornbread along with the canned goods and onions. As the platters of cornbread got low, Sarah Lee would bring in fresh platters with more buttermilk. All of the guests were getting full of food and buttermilk and were pushing their plates away. Granddaddy again apologized for the meal and began to ring the dinner bell. Three kitchen helpers appeared and cleaned up the table. Sarah Lee and her assistants arrived at the table with silver, china, glasses and napkins, placing them in front of each guest. Behind Sarah Lee, the three helpers from the kitchen arrived with platters in both hands, filled with baked turkey, pork roast, roast beef, butter beans, snap beans, rice and gravy, creamed corn, peas, fried chicken, hot rolls, and an assortment of jellies and jams.

Granddaddy told the guests to help themselves and to eat all they wanted. Iced tea was served, along with steaming cups of coffee. All the guests could do was to moan and rub their stomachs.

Mr. Lyons said, "Dick, you have pulled another one of your tricks. We are all so full of buttermilk and canned goods, that it is doubtful we will be able to eat for several days, much less eat any of the wonderful food placed before us."

The hunting crowd had hardly arrived back in Mobile before everyone was approaching them, asking if old Captain Dick had fed them before leaving Finchburg.

These were not the first or last of his many jokes.

About the Author

R. B. "Dickie" Williams III was born in Mobile, Alabama, on Jan. 2, 1935. His family moved to Monroeville in 1937, and during World War II, while his father was in the Navy, he, his mother, and his brother Robbins, lived in Tunnel Springs with his grandparents, Mr. and Mrs. C. J. Jackson. But summers and holidays were spent with his Granddaddy Williams on the Williams plantation in Finchburg, Alabama, 18 miles west of Tunnel Springs.

He went to summer school in Beatrice, eight miles north of Tunnel Springs. He graduated from Monroeville High School in 1953, where he lettered four years in football, basketball, and baseball. He enrolled at Auburn in 1953, then transferred to Howard College (now Samford University) where he graduated in 1958 with a B.S. in pharmacy.

He worked at Edgewood Drug Store in Homewood while in school and several months after graduating, then moved to Selma, Alabama, in late 1958 and worked there at Swift Drug Co. He joined the Dixie Division of the National Guard and served six months active duty at Ft. Jackson, S.C. In 1960, he married Sue Russell from Safford, Alabama. In August 1961, he moved back to Monroeville and opened Williams Drug Store, which he has run since. In his spare time, he organized and created the Monroe County Conservation Club, the Monroe County Museum, and the Monroe County State Fishing Lake at Beatrice, Alabama. He has served as president of the Alabama Wildlife Federation and has been elected as Alabama delegate to the National Wildlife Federation for 21 consecutive years.

His advice to all: "Press on and don't sweat the little things."